Research in the Wild

Synthesis Lectures on Human-Centered Informatics

Editor
John M. Carroll, *Penn State University*

Human-Centered Informatics (HCI) is the intersection of the cultural, the social, the cognitive, and the aesthetic with computing and information technology. It encompasses a huge range of issues, theories, technologies, designs, tools, environments, and human experiences in knowledge work, recreation and leisure activity, teaching and learning, and the potpourri of everyday life. The series publishes state-of-the-art syntheses, case studies, and tutorials in key areas. It shares the focus of leading international conferences in HCI.

Research in the Wild
Yvonne Rogers and Paul Marshall
April 2017

Designing for Gesture and Tangible Interaction
Mary Lou Maher and Lina Lee
March 2017

From Tool to Partner: The Evolution of Human-Computer Interaction
Jonathan Grudin
December 2016

Qualitative HCI Research: Going behind the Scenes
Ann Blandford, Dominic Furniss, and Stephann Makri
April 2016

Learner-Centered Design of Computing Education: Research on Computing for Everyone
Mark Guzdial
November 2015

The Envisionment and Discovery Collaboratory (EDC): Explorations in Human-Centered Informatics with Tabletop Computing Environments
Ernesto G. Arias, Hal Eden, and Gerhard Fischer
October 2015

Research in the Wild
Yvonne Rogers and Paul Marshall

ISBN: 978-3-031-01092-7 print
ISBN: 978-3-031-02220-3 ebook
DOI 10.1007/978-3-031-02220-3

A Publication in the Springer series
SYNTHESIS LECTURES ON HUMAN-CENTERED INFORMATICS, #37

Series Editors: John M. Carroll, Penn State University

Series ISSN: 1946-7680 Print   1946-7699 Electronic

Research in the Wild

Yvonne Rogers and Paul Marshall
University College London

SYNTHESIS LECTURES ON HUMAN-CENTERED INFORMATICS #37

ABSTRACT

The phrase "in-the-wild" is becoming popular again in the field of human-computer interaction (HCI), describing approaches to HCI research and accounts of user experience phenomena that differ from those derived from other lab-based methods. The phrase first came to the forefront 20–25 years ago when anthropologists Jean Lave (1988), Lucy Suchman (1987), and Ed Hutchins (1995) began writing about cognition being in-the-wild. Today, it is used more broadly to refer to research that seeks to understand new technology interventions in everyday living.

A reason for its resurgence in contemporary HCI is an acknowledgment that so much technology is now embedded and used in our everyday lives. Researchers have begun following suit—decamping from their usability and living labs and moving into the wild; carrying out *in-situ* development and engagement, sampling experiences, and probing people in their homes and on the streets.

The aim of this book is to examine what this new direction entails and what it means for HCI theory, practice, and design. The focus is on the insights, demands and concerns. But how does research in the wild differ from the other applied approaches in interaction design, such as contextual design, action research, or ethnography? What is added by labeling user research as being in-the-wild? One main difference is where the research starts and ends: unlike user-centered, and more specifically, ethnographic approaches which typically begin by observing existing practices and then suggesting general design implications or system requirements, in-the-wild approaches create and evaluate new technologies and experiences *in situ* (Rogers, 2012). Moreover, novel technologies are often developed to augment people, places, and settings, without necessarily designing them for specific user needs. There has also been a shift in design thinking. Instead of developing solutions that fit in with existing practices, researchers are experimenting with new technological possibilities that can change and even disrupt behavior. Opportunities are created, interventions installed, and different ways of behaving are encouraged. A key concern is how people react, change and integrate these in their everyday lives. This book outlines the emergence and development of research in the wild. It is structured around a framework for conceptualizing and bringing together the different strands. It covers approaches, methods, case studies, and outcomes. Finally, it notes that there is more in the wild research in HCI than usability and other kinds of user studies in HCI and what the implications of this are for the field.

KEYWORDS

human-computer interaction, HCI, *in situ* studies, research in the wild

Contents

Acknowledgments

We would like to thank Eva Hornecker, Jesper Kjeldskov, and Erik Stolterman for their insightful comments on an earlier draft. We would also like to thank all our colleagues at Sussex University, Open University, and University College London who collaborated with us in our forays into the wild.

CHAPTER 1

Introduction

1.1 RESEARCH GONE WILD

It is now quite common to see the phrase "in the wild" inserted into the title of a human-computer interaction (HCI) paper. Examples include "Doing innovation in the wild" (Crabtree et al., 2013a), "Being in the thick of in the wild" (Johnson et al., 2012), and "A robot in the wild" (Williams et al., 2014), as well as abbreviated versions such as "Leaving the wild" (Taylor et al., 2013) and "Calls from the wild" (Cappadonna et al., 2016). Besides attracting eyeballs ("the wild" sounds more intriguing than the more prosaic "An *in situ* study of..." or "An Investigation into...") this trend reflects a shift in how research is being carried out in HCI. Increasingly, researchers are going into people's homes, the outdoors, and public places, to study their reactions to, use, and appropriation of a diversity of technologies that researchers have provided them with or placed in that location. Examples include exploring the co-creation of a street graph depicting changes in electricity consumption for a community (Bird and Rogers, 2010), the use of mobile devices for tracking people's health (Consolvo et al., 2008), and exploring how robots can assist the well-being of visitors in hospital wards (e.g., Dahl and Bolous, 2014). In addition, researchers are working and participating more with communities, designing and deploying technologies *in situ* that address the latter's concerns or needs. Theory has also been rethought in terms of how it can inform, extend, or develop accounts of behavior that is *situated* in naturalistic settings and in the context of *socio-technical* practices.

Research in the wild (RITW) is generally considered as an umbrella term to refer to how, what, and where research is conducted in naturalistic settings (Crabtree et al., 2013b). *Its overarching goal is to understanding how technology is and can be used in the everyday/real world, in order to gain new insights about: how to engage people/communities in various activities, how people's lives are impacted by a specific technology, and what people do when encountering a new technology in a given setting.* The output can be used to inform the development of new understandings, theories, or concepts about human behavior in the real world. This includes rethinking cognitive theories, in terms of ecological concepts (e.g., situated memory) and socio-cultural accounts (e.g., the effects of digitalization on society). More specifically, RITW can be concerned with investigating an assumption, such as whether or not a technology intervention can encourage people to change a behavior (e.g., exercising more). It can be operationalized in terms of a research question to be evaluated in the wild, such as: will providing free activity trackers to employees to encourage them to develop new social practices at work (e.g., buddying up, competing with each other) that will help them to become fitter and healthier? The perspective taken for this kind of RITW is to observe how people react, change and integrate the technology in question into their everyday lives over a period of time.

RITW is broad in its scope. Some have questioned the need for yet another term for what many HCI researchers would claim they have been doing for years. Indeed, applied research has been an integral part of HCI, addressing real-world problems, by conducting field studies, user studies and ethnographies. The outputs of which are intended to inform system design, often through community engagement. So, what is the value of coining another label? We would argue that, first, it is now widely used not just in HCI, but also in a number of other disciplines, including biology and psychology, reflecting a growing trend towards pursuing more research in naturalistic settings. Second, the term is more encompassing, covering a wider range of research compared with other kinds of named methodological approaches, such as Action Research, Participatory Design, or Research Through Design. Initial ethnographic research, followed by designing a new user experience, together with the application and/or development of theory, technology innovation, and an *in situ* evaluation study are often conducted all in one RITW project.

Hence, while the various components involved in RITW are not new, a single project often addresses several of them. Rather than focus on one aspect, e.g., developing a new technology, advancing a new method, testing the effects of a variable or reporting on the findings of a technology intervention—research in the wild typically combines a number of interlinked strands. Technology innovation can initially inspire the design of a new learning activity that in parallel is framed in terms of a particular theory of learning. Together, they inform the design of an *in situ* study and the research questions it will address.

RITW is agnostic about the methods, technologies, or theories it uses. Accordingly, it does not necessarily follow one kind of methodology, where one design phase follows another, but combines different ones to address a problem/concern or opportunity, as deemed fit. Sometimes, theory might be considered central and other times only marginal; sometimes, "off-the-shelf" technology is deployed and evaluated in an *in situ* study. Other times, the design and deployment of a novel device is the focus. In other settings, the focus of a project is how best to work alongside a community so that a democratic design process is followed.

The multiple decisions that have to be made when operationalizing a problem are often the main drivers, shaping how the proposed research will address identified questions, what methods/technologies to use and what can be learned. In summary, RITW is broadly conceived, accommodating a diversity of methodologies, epistemologies and ways of doing research. What is common to all RITW projects is the importance placed on the setting and context, conducting research in the everyday and in naturalistic environments.

1.2   HOW DOES RESEARCH IN THE WILD DIFFER FROM LAB EXPERIMENTS?

A long-standing debate in HCI is concerned with what is lost and gained when moving research out of a controlled lab setting into the wild (Preece et al., 2015). An obvious benefit is more ecological validity—an *in situ* study is likely to reveal more the kinds of problems and behaviors people will have and adopt if they were to use a novel device at home, at work, or elsewhere. A lab study is less likely to show these aspects as participants try to work out what to do in order to complete the tasks set for them, by following instructions given. They may find themselves having to deal with various "demand characteristics"—the cues that make them aware of what the experimenter expects to find, wants to happen or how they are expected to behave. As such, ecological validity of lab studies can be less reliable, as participants perform to conform to the experimenter's expectations.

A downside of evaluating technology in situ, however, is the researcher losing control over how it will be used or interacted with. Tasks can be set in a lab and predictions made to investigate systematically how participants manage to do them, when using a novel device, system, or app. When in the wild, however, participants are typically given a device to use without any set tasks provided. They may be told what it can do and given instructions on how to use it but the purpose of evaluating it in a naturalistic setting is to explore what happens when they try to use it in this context—where there may be other demands and factors at play. However, this can often mean that only a fraction of the full range of functionality, that has been designed as part of the technology, is used or explored, making it difficult for the researchers to see whether what has been designed is useful, usable, or capable of supporting the intended interactions.

To examine how much is lost and gained, Kjeldskov et al. (2004) conducted a comparative study of a mobile system designed for nurses in the lab vs. in the wild. They found that both settings revealed similar kinds of usability problems but that more were discovered in the lab than in the wild study. However, the cost of running a study in the wild was considerably greater than in the lab, leading them to question "Was it worth the hassle?" They suggest that in the wild studies might be better suited for obtaining initial insights for how to design a new system that can then feed into the requirements gathering process, while early usability testing of a prototype system can be done in the confines of the lab. This pragmatic approach to usability testing and requirements gathering makes good sense when considering how best to develop and progress a new system design. In a follow-up survey of research on mobile HCI using lab and in the wild studies, Kjeldskov and Skov (2014) concluded that it is not a matter of one being better than the other but when best to conduct a lab study vs. an in the wild study. Furthermore, they conclude that when researchers go into the wild they should "go all the way" and not settle for some "half-tame" setting. Only by carrying out truly wild studies can researchers experience and understand real-world use.

Findings from other RITW user studies have shown how they can reveal a lot more than identifying usability problems (Hornecker and Nicol, 2012). In particular, they enable researchers to explore how a range of factors can influence user behavior *in situ*—in terms of how people notice, approach, and decide what to do with a technology intervention—either one they are given to try or one they come across—that goes beyond the scope of what is typically able to be observed in a lab-based study. Rogers et al. (2007) found marked differences in usability and usefulness when comparing a mobile device in the wild and in the lab; the mobile device was developed to enable groups of students to carry out environmental science, as part of a long-term project investigating ecological restoration of urban regions. The device provided interactive software that allowed a user to record and look up relevant data, information visualizations, and statistics. The device was intended to replace the existing practice of using a paper-based method of recording measurements of tree growth when in the field. Placing the new mobile device in the palms of students on a cold spring day revealed a whole host of unexpected, context-based usability and user experience problems. Placing the device in the palms of students on a hot summer day revealed a quite different set of unexpected, context-based usability and user experience problems. The device was used quite differently for the different times of year, where foliage and other environmental cues vary and affect the extent to which a tree can be found and identified.

Other studies have also found how people will often approach and use prototypes differently in the wild compared with in a lab setting (e.g., Brown et al., 2011; Peltonen et al., 2008; van der Linden et al., 2011). People are often inventive and creative in what they do when coming across a prototype or system, but also can get frustrated or confused, in ways that are difficult to predict or expect from lab-based studies (Marshall et al., 2011). Van der Linden et al. (2011) also observed different behaviors—not evident from their lab-based studies—when investigating how haptic technology could improve children's learning to play the violin at school. An *in situ* study of their Music-Jacket system showed how real-time vibrotactile feedback was most effective when matched to tasks selected by their teachers to be at the right level of difficulty—rather than what the researchers thought would be right for them. Similarly, Gallacher et al. (2015) discovered quite different findings when they ran the same in the wild study in different places. Based on the differing outcomes from lab studies and in in the wild approaches, Rogers et al. (2013) questioned whether findings from controlled settings can transfer to real-world settings.

In summary, *in situ* studies can provide new ways of thinking about how to scope and conduct research. Compared with running experiments and usability studies, where researchers try to predict in advance performance and the likelihood or kind of usability errors, running *in situ* studies nearly always provide unexpected findings about what humans might or might not do when confronted with a new technology intervention. Even when experiments are run in the wild, non-significant findings can be most informative. Part of the appeal of RITW is uncovering the unexpected rather than confirming what is hoped for or already known.

1.3   A FRAMEWORK FOR HCI RESEARCH IN THE WILD

RITW is eclectic in what it does and what it seeks to understand. Such an unstructured approach to research might seem unwieldy, lacking the rigor and commitment usually associated with a given epistemology. However, this broad church stance does not mean sloppiness or lowering of standards; rather, it can open up new possibilities for conducting far-reaching, impactful, and innovative research. To help frame RITW we have developed a generic framework. Figure 1.1 depicts RITW in terms of four core bases that connect to each other. These are regarded as starting places from which to scope and operationalize the research, in terms of:

1. technology,

2. design,

3. *in situ* studies, and

4. theory.

Each can inform the others to situate, shape, and progress the research. For example, *designing* a new activity (e.g., collaborative learning) can be done by working alongside others (e.g., participatory design), leading to the development of a new *technology*. The findings from an *in situ* study (e.g., how people search for information on the fly using their smartphones) can inform new *theory* (e.g., augmented memory). An existing theory (e.g., attention) can inform the design of a new app intended to be used to measure how people multitask in their everyday lives when using smartphones, tablets, and laptops. The design of a new *technology* (e.g., augmented reality) can be used to enhance a social activity in the wild (e.g., how families learn about the ecology of woodlands together). It should be stressed, however, that the RITW framework is not meant to be prescriptive, in terms of which base to start from, or what methods and analytic lens to use, when conducting research. The selection of these depends on the motivation for the research, its scoping, the available funding and resources, and expected outcomes.

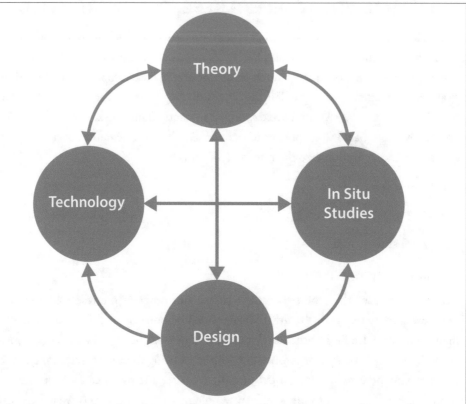

Technology: Concerned with appropriating existing infrastructures/devices (e.g., Internet of Things toolkit, mobile app) *in situ* or developing new ones for a given setting (e.g., a novel public display).

Design: Covers the design space of an experience (e.g., iteratively creating a collaborative travel planning tool for families to use or an augmented reality game for playing outdoors).

***In situ* study:** Concerned with evaluating *in situ* an existing device/tool/service or novel research-based prototype when placed in various settings or given to someone to use over a period of time.

Theory: Investigating a theory, idea, concept or observation about a behavior, setting or other phenomenon using existing ones or developing a new one or extending an existing one.

Figure 1.1: Research in the wild (RITW) framework.

1.4 SCOPING RESEARCH IN THE WILD

There are many ways of conducting research in the wild. An initial challenge is to scope the research to determine what can be realistically discovered or demonstrated, which methods to use to achieve this and what to expect when using them. Sometimes, it might involve deploying hundreds of prototypes in people's homes (e.g., Gaver et al., 2016) to observe the varied adoptions and appropriations of many people rather than those of a few. Other times, it entails months of community-building and stakeholder engagement in order to build up trust and commitment before studying the outcome of an intervention they propose or a disruption on behavior (e.g., changing habits to enable communities to reduce their energy or increase their exercise). In other contexts, it can involve running a longitudinal study across geographical boundaries to determine how new tools encourage participation in different cultures, such as citizen science projects. The scoping will depend a lot on practical concerns, such as how much funding is available, the time of year, logistics and gaining the trust of and acceptance in a community in order to get people on board to see the potential value of a proposed technology.

A number of methods are typically used in RITW, including observation, surveys, remote logging of people's use of technology (e.g., monitoring their activity), and engagement with community members in a variety of contexts through the use of focus groups, co-design sessions, and town hall meetings—in order to hear their opinions and let them voice their concerns. Data that is collected using different methods is typically aggregated to provide a combination of quantitative and qualitative results. However, collecting multiple streams of data over several months can quickly multiply the outputs, making it difficult to tease out what might be causing particular effects or why people behave (or not) in certain ways. Much skill is involved in making sense of the different kinds of data without jumping to conclusions. There may be many factors and interdependencies at play that might be causing the observed effects or observed phenomena.

Despite this increase in uncertainty and lack of control, what is discovered and interpreted from RITW can be most revealing about what happens in the real world (Rogers et al., 2007; Marshall et al., 2011; Hornecker and Nicol, 2012). A benefit of RITW is greater ecological validity compared with extrapolating results from lab studies. Most significantly, RITW studies can show how people understand and appropriate technologies in their own terms and for their own situated purposes. Accordingly, RITW is increasingly being used to show 'impact' in terms of how new interventions have made a difference to a community (e.g., Balestrini et al., 2017), or how in the wild findings can provide empirical evidence for changing behavior or policy in society.

Thought Box: Beyond the Interface

Even though many of us still struggle to get the proverbial photocopier to copy (indeed our computer science department was offering tutorials to all staff, from professors to Ph.D. students, earlier this year with the arrival of a new machine), the pressing problems HCI researchers are increasingly concerned with are how people interact with an ecology of interfaces. A *core challenge is to enable people to be able to switch between multiple interfaces and multiple devices.* This framing requires understanding the context for why and how someone moves between them. Rather than being concerned with how best to support X (where X might be learning, working, socializing) using an individual device (e.g., a laptop, tablet or smartphone) it is necessary to work out how to design across platforms so that people can fluidly use multiple tools and devices, as they go about their everyday lives—picking up one, putting another down, or using several together in unison, by themselves or when interacting with others (Coughlan et al., 2012). What might seem obvious to do in a lab setting may not be obvious and may even be counter-intuitive in a real-world setting. A question this raises is how to frame, and which methods to use, when researching such multi-device settings across time and place in the wild?

1.5   AIM OF THE BOOK

The aim of this book is to provide an overview of HCI research in the wild, illustrating how it can traverse theory, design, technology, and *in situ* studies. It covers the motivations, concerns, methods and outcomes. As part of this endeavor, it addresses the challenges of conducting RITW, including the questions asked, the expectations, the trade-offs, the uncertainties, the form of analyses adopted, the role of the researcher, and their conduct when in the wild settings.

The book is targeted at both students and researchers who are new to the field of HCI and more generally, research methods, or for someone who simply wants to learn more about research in the wild. It covers RITW by charting and critiquing the what, when, where, why and how questions. In subsequent parts of the book, it examines the tools, methods, and platforms that have been imported, adapted and developed to study user-interactions in the wild, and how researchers have grounded concerns, problems, and new opportunities through their framing. It also outlines the benefits, limitations, impacts, and advances that have resulted from research in the wild.

1.6   SUMMARY

One of the motivations for conducting research in the wild is to demonstrate how a technology intervention can engage a community in a participatory manner. Underlying motivations include enabling people to collaborate, connect with each other or join forces in order to raise awareness, and act upon an issue. Another rationale for conducting RITW is to deploy novel technologies in a setting in order to provoke a response (e.g., getting people to comment on a new display in a street), a new kind of interaction (exploring how one looks in an augmented public mirror) or social engagement (e.g., encouraging strangers to talk with one another in a public place). A further reason is to develop new understandings and theorizing about how people use technology in their everyday lives—based on the body of empirical work that demonstrates how behavior differs or is the same as when using "older" and other kinds of technologies. In summary, RITW is becoming more widely accepted as a de facto way of conducting research for HCI, complimenting but also questioning the validity of traditional lab-based research approaches.

CHAPTER 2

Moving Into The Wild: From Situated Cognition to Embodied Interaction

2.1 INTRODUCTION

The phrase "in the wild" first came to the forefront, in the late 1980s and early 1990s when anthropologists Lucy Suchman (1987), Jean Lave (1988), and Ed Hutchins (1995) began writing about cognition in the wild. Collectively, they critiqued the fledgling field of cognitive science, which was concerned with how the mind worked. The accepted theorizing at the time focused on information processing in the head, and the construction of rational models of behavior as the execution of plans. In sharp contrast to this classical view, they explain cognition—as observed in everyday practice—being distributed and situated in the moment. Moreover, in their respective books (see Figure 2.1), they cogently argue that cognition can only be studied in the wild. Their approach was to present a social anthropology of cognition and cognition in practice, respectively.

Figure 2.1: Suchman's, Lave's, and Hutchins' classic "In the Wild" books.

2.2   PLANS AND SITUATED ACTION

The first in the wild classic was Lucy Suchman's (1987) *Plans and Situated Actions* book. It took the fields of HCI and computer science by storm—and its insights were quickly adopted by a new generation of researchers and students. For many, it resonated with their discontent and worries about the limitations of traditional cognitive models. For others, it opened their eyes to new ways of thinking about human-machine interactions. The accepted view at the time was that scientific models were needed to explain how the mind works and that these should form the basis of user models used in machine-human dialogues. Folk theories or common sense explanations were dismissed as inadequate. Suchman, however, argued the opposite: *common sense* notions of planning should *not* be viewed as inadequate versions of scientific models of action, but taken as resources people use in their practical deliberations. To support her contrarian view of how to conceptualize and understand human behavior, she described how people use these resources along with various constraints in the environment in their everyday planning and action. Instead of developing so called scientific models to develop human-computer interfaces, developers should draw from accounts of how people act and react in their everyday lives.

Much of Suchman's early research was to provide detailed situated accounts of the relations among people and between people and technology. One of her most cited examples is of a study she conducted of pairs of users trying to fathom out how to use a Xerox photocopier. While not an in the wild study (since it was conducted in a Xerox Research lab), she noted how its complicated help system did not match the way the pairs understood how it worked or what to do when it did not work in the way they thought it should. The outcome of her detailed analyses of the mismatched photocopier-user interactions led many programmers and developers to rethink how they should structure and what to include in their human-computer models, replacing the simplified process models, that followed sets of rules, such as "if x then y" with alternative kinds of situated models of action (Dourish, 2001).

An analogy that she used in her book to illustrate what she meant by situated action is a description of what it is like to ride the rapids in a canoe. She notes how a great deal of deliberation and reconstruction goes into a canoeist's plan both before they begin and in their account of what happened after the event, but from then how they actually navigate the rapids, depends on embodied skills in responding to whatever comes their way. This powerful image resonated with many as to why models of plans as a control structure that specify behavior were inadequate when designing user interfaces. Despite its impact on a generation of researchers, however, this example, itself, has been somewhat parodied and often misunderstood. Many took it to mean plans are irrelevant to how we act. Suchman never claimed this (and goes to great length to explain what she meant in her later revised version of the book), arguing that what happens in practice is the interaction of both the contingencies and the projected course of action. A legacy from her pioneering work is the commonly accepted view that users don't follow instructions and plans as simply as had been assumed.

2.3   COGNITION IN PRACTICE

Jean Lave's (1988) book *Cognition in Practice*, published a year later, was primarily concerned with debunking the academic snobbery associated with "common sense explanations and real-world contexts." Similar to Suchman's critique of cognitive science models of everyday planning, she went to great lengths to explain how experimental lab research wasn't superior to everyday people's accounts of what they do in their lives. Moreover, her program of research showed how it was more valuable and legitimate to study people's cognitive behavior in everyday contexts, which she described as "cognition in the wild." To demonstrate how her approach could provide new understandings, she studied adults practicing math in a variety of real-world contexts. Some of the examples she described in her book, which are most illuminating, are of people working out the best price for groceries when shopping in the supermarket and for how dieters measure unusual quantities of ingredients when making a dish at home while following a recipe. Similar to Suchman's book, she compellingly demonstrates, through her detailed case studies, how people often use opportunistic structures in the real world in their everyday cognition.

The legacy of Lave's work was to show how it was possible and necessary to move one particular form of cognitive activity—arithmetic problem-solving—out of the laboratory back into the realm of everyday life. In so doing, she showed how mathematics in the real world is the same for all kinds of thinking, shaped by the reflexive encounter between human minds and the context people find themselves in. A salient example that has been much cited—as illustrative of doing math in practice—is the "cottage cheese" problem; a male dieter, preparing a meal, was faced with having to measure out 3/4 of 2/3 of a cup of cottage cheese that was stipulated in the recipe he was using. How did he work it out? Not by multiplying 3 x 2 and dividing that by 4 x 3, resulting in ½, as would be expected if using algebra in school, but instead by using the available structures in the environment in a situated way. He first measured out 2/3 of a cup, and then spread it on a chopping board in the shape of a circle. Next, he divided the circle into 4 quarters, removed one of them and returned it to the container, leaving on the board the desired 3/4 of 2/3 a cup.

Similar to Suchman's canoe example, the dieter example of using external resources to solve a math problem paved the way for rethinking cognition in practice rather than in abstraction, and the insight that mathematics is *for* something; the mathematical abstractions taught in schools don't necessarily transfer well to use outside the classroom. A number of other examples in Lave's book are used to emphasize how people use the resources from the context they are in to solve problems. Together, the examples convincingly demonstrate how activities in settings are complex improvisations that have much variability. Doing math when out there takes a different form in different situations. One of the outcomes of this early form of in the wild research was to make studying everyday and common sense reasoning acceptable, by giving it credibility and respectability (cf. Rogers, 1993).

2.4   COGNITION IN THE WILD

Ed Hutchins published *Cognition in the Wild* a few years later in 1995. His seminal book was also very much a reaction against the status quo; but more broadly than either Lucy Suchman's or Jean Lave's efforts. His beef was very much a rally against "cognition in captivity" and "disembodied cognition." He argued that much of mainstream thinking about cognitive science for the past 30 years had resulted in systematic distortions of our understanding of the nature of cognition. Instead, he proposed that cognition should be studied in its natural habitat and that, in doing so, it would change our ideas about its nature. He argued that what was problematic with the classical cognitive science approach, was not its conceptual framework *per se*, but its exclusive focus on modeling the cognitive processes that occurred within one individual. As an alternative, he argued that what was needed was for the same conceptual framework to be applied to a range of cognitive systems, including socio-technical systems at large (i.e., groups of individual agents interacting with each other in particular environments). To do this, he proposed studying cognition beyond the skin of the individual, encompassing the distributed nature of cognitive phenomena across individuals, artifacts, and internal and external representations.

Hutchins also argued that in order to reveal the properties and processes of such a cognitive system required conducting an ethnographic study of a setting. Paying close attention to the activities of people and their interactions with material media was considered fundamental to understanding how such a cognitive system works. Hutchins' intricate analyses of what happens inside a cognitive system at both the micro and macro levels were at the time groundbreaking. One of his most well known examples is an account of how the cockpit plus air traffic control tower system work together as a cognitive system. He illustrates this eloquently by describing the joint activity and accomplishment of a situation when a pilot and co-pilot fly their plane to a higher altitude in conjunction with listening to and talking with air traffic controllers. It demonstrates just how much coordinated activity depends on the orchestration of mechanisms through which co-located and distributed people make small signals to each other in order to progress a sequenced activity, and the levels of inter-subjectivity involved for different states of the system. A missed cue can easily result in a misunderstanding, especially if someone is not expecting it. These can happen even for the most routine of activities which then requires the cognitive system to engage in various forms of repair work and sometimes the adoption of workarounds to get the activity back on track.

The legacy of the distributed cognition approach is its demonstration of how insightful it can be to analyze the complex interdependencies between people and artifacts in their work activities—

which is often overlooked in other kinds of cognitive analyses. Hutchins approach to "cognition in the wild" clearly showed how important micro-analyses can be to reveal the multi-layered work that a cognitive system has to do—and where subtle actions, such as a glance, a gesture, or a flick of a switch at a particular time, are often integral to the coordination and mediation of teamwork.

2.5   EMBODIED INTERACTION APPROACHES

Since these early pioneering "in the wild" theory books, there have been further writings in HCI and cognitive science that have stressed the importance of understanding the ways people are closely coupled with their environment. These include seminal works that view interaction as embodied (Dourish, 2001), cognition as external (Scaife and Rogers, 1996), and perception as enactive (Noë, 2004). In the 2000s, and to this day, conceptualizing human-computer interactions as embodied in real-world contexts has become an influential approach (Marshall et al., 2013). In its broadest sense, embodied interaction refers to the "everyday, mundane experience" (Dourish, 2001, p. 125) and the ways that people understand the world through their accomplishment of practical activities. However, many questions remain as to exactly what it means in practice and whether it can be considered a coherent program of research in HCI.

Many of the ideas about embodied interaction, which have been developed in HCI, built upon the phenomenological ideas of Husserl, Merleau-Ponty, and Heidegger. These earlier philosophical writings were largely concerned with the essence of what it means to be, to see, to have a conscience and be aware of the world. The "lived" experiences were accounted for in terms of many aspects, but primarily in terms of space, time, and what it means to live in the world. Likewise, McCarthy and Wright's (2004) influential *Technology as Experience* framework, concerned with the "felt" experience of being in the world, was based on phenomenology, and in particular, the writings of John Dewey and Mikhail Bakhtin. Instead of describing HCI in terms of how usable a device or interface is, they argued for explaining user's interaction with technology more in terms of their *felt experience*, i.e., how something is felt by them. In so doing, they make the case for understanding users in terms of their whole experience of a technology, especially how they makes sense of it in the context of use, by considering the emotional, intellectual, and sensual aspects of their interactions with technology. This stance emphasizes the importance of understanding how people do not just use technology, but that they also live with it.

Contemporary philosophers have also become interested in understanding cognition in the world. Particularly notable, is Andy Clark and David Chalmers' (1998) "Extended Mind" hypothesis—the underlying idea being that the mind does not have to be contained within the brain or physical body, but can be extended to elements of the environment. The hypothesis suggests how technology continues to extend and increase what humans are capable of doing, enabling them to make more rapid decisions, understand complex situations, and find solutions to difficult problems.

Since, Clark and Chalmers ideas have been taken up and elaborated by other philosophers, including Ward and Stapleton's (2012) provocative paper, "Es are good. Cognition as enacted, embodied, embedded, affective and extended." A central idea is that tools and artifacts are absorbed into the body schema, extending and changing it. An example that is often used to illustrate this idea of extended cognition is the blind man with his stick—where the stick becomes an extension of his arm/hand, extending the boundary of the space surrounding his body and perception of the world.

Alva Noë (2009) also wrote cogently about how perception is not like looking at pictures in the mind; instead we perceive the world by gradual active inquiry and exploration of it. A central tenet of his position is that given that we spend all our lives embodied and situated in the world around us, it follows that our perceptual experiences are acquired through our bodily experiences with the world. Hence, it does not make sense to understand the mind, consciousness, or problem-solving as something that occurs in the brain. We are in the moment in a shared context—whether it is a football match, having dinner together, or engaged in banter on social media. A challenge is how to take into account this context when designing new technologies to aid, augment, or provide new opportunities for cognition, social interactions or cultural experiences.

Technologies, such as augmented reality, virtual reality, and haptic feedback, have been able to provide philosophers with new interactive tools with which to investigate and validate embodied theories of body/mind. For example, Bird et al. (2009) explored how they could design tactile interfaces to mediate novel sensory information to enable people to experience the technology as an extension of themselves. Conversely, theories about embodied and the extended mind can inform the design of technologies that extend what humans can perceive and do in the world. For example, technologies have been designed to provide users with extended ways of perceiving the world, such as "Sixthsense" (Misty and Maes, 2009), which was a demonstration of a wearable gestural interface intended to augment the physical world with digital information that could be interacted with using natural hand gestures.

Both approaches can inform new theories about augmented cognition while also providing empirical evidence for embodied theories (cf. Rogers, 2011). For example, David Kirsh (2013) notes how, "*The theory of embodied cognition offers us new ways to think about bodies, mind, and technology. Designing interactivity will never be the same.*" He illustrates this bold claim with his research on how dancers use their bodies when rehearsing: where he demonstrated how they are able to learn and consolidate mastery of a complex dance phrase better by physically practicing a simplified but distorted model than by mentally simulating it undistorted (Kirsh, 2014). The idea that we think with our bodies, not just our brains, that in turn shapes how we think and solve problems is profound and has important implications for how we think about designing cognitive tools to think with and augment human behavior.

2.6   CURRENT THEORIZING WITHIN RESEARCH IN THE WILD

Whereas the anthropologists and philosophers' alternative theories of *cognition in the wild* were largely pitted against cognitive psychology and cognitive science theories, that were mainstream at the time, today's HCI researchers are largely concerned with *technology in the wild*, with no particular discipline to put to right. While a few sociologists, who had ventured into the field of HCI in the 1990s, railed against having any kind of theory about cognition, including a damning critique of Hutchins *Cognition in the Wild* (Button, 2008), many others embraced the ideas of explaining cognition as situated or distributed across technology, people, and artifacts—leading them to develop new conceptual frameworks from which to account for, analyze, and inform the design of situated technologies (e.g., Rogers and Ellis, 1994; Rogers, 1992; Halverson, 2002; Hollan et al., 2000; Furniss and Blandford, 2006; Liu et al., 2008).

At the same time, HCI research in the wild continues to discover how established theories of human cognition, largely derived from research conducted in the lab, are not adequate accounts of real-world behavior. A number of HCI researchers have found that old school cognitive and social theories do not describe or adequately account for how people interact with technology in their everyday lives, especially when considering how digital technologies and physical artifacts have now become so entwined in what people say, do, think, or remember (Rogers, 2012). For example, Bergman and Whittaker's (2016) research on personal information management shows that classical theories of information management do not match up with how people actually manage their "digital stuff." In contrast, based on their body of empirical work of what happens in the real world, they propose an alternative three-stage model of personal information management, where curation is viewed as being at the core of how people store, retrieve, manage, and exploit their data —be it via their phone, computer, laptop, or other device. They suggest this alternative theorizing can provide new insights and principles for how to design new digital management and navigation tools—that differ from existing approaches, such as tagging, searching, and grouping. Furthermore, they point out how people's curation behaviors persist over time—despite changes in the technological devices they use, together with the exponential growth of digital content they create, keep, and want access to. Many of the problems people have organizing, storing and re-accessing their email are the same ones they have with their photos, personal data, or files. We are creatures of habit and they argue we need to design our technologies accordingly—rather than take existing theories of how to optimize information management/retrieval.

While the situated, distributed, and embodied theories have provided new understandings and framings of human activity in the real world, they only go so far. What is also needed, besides new theories of cognition to replace the old classical ones (cf. to Bergman and Whittaker's approach, 2016), is to rethink theory more broadly, both at macro and micro level of analyses, to account for how people are using, relying on, and appropriating the diversity of technologies that have become suffused in their lives.

One way to achieve this is to explore the interdependences between design, technology, and behavior. While this approach is not new—for example, socio-technical systems theories has been around for years—the subject of interest is, i.e., theorizing about people's everyday use and interactions with technologies and their environment. Another way is to begin theorizing about how digitalization, in its various manifestations, is affecting society. For example, consider the growing concern in society about whether children's reading skills are declining. In particular, a question has been raised as to whether the practice of bedtime reading (which is considered instrumental to helping children learn to read independently) is changing through the widespread take up of interactive ebooks and tablets. A study conducted by Nicola Yuill and Alex Martin (2016) investigated how to operationalize the wider context of understanding children's reading skills. They wanted to know if it matters whether a traditional paper book or a tablet screen is used for bedtime reading. Are there differences in their affordances and properties that affects the age old practice of parents and their children reading a bedtime story together? To answer this, they carried out a controlled experiment in a naturalistic setting. They came up with a number of indices to describe when children are reading and being read to, in order to see if there were any differences between shared reading of digital and paper texts. The measures they used were for: *cognitive aspects* (e.g., do they differ in their attentional engagement), *interactive and affective aspects* (e.g., are there differences in the warmth of mother-child interactions when reading screen and paper media?), and *postural aspects* (are there differences in the physical positioning of mother and child when reading from screens vs. paper?).

The experimental design drew heavily from developmental theory and experimental design. The *theory* of joint attention was used to frame the design of the study to explore these aspects. An *in situ* study was then conducted to answer the questions—by observing and recording the joint attention between parents and children when sitting on a sofa together in their own homes reading a book at bedtime. Much thought went into the selection of the participants, the materials used, and the length of reading with the use of a repeated-measures design, using four conditions (Mother-Paper, Child-Paper, Mother-Digital, Child-Digital).

Reading errors and recall of material were collected and then coded, providing specific measures of richness of description and narrative coherence. The findings from the study revealed a number of differences, for example, they found that reading interactions involving a screen showed slightly lower warmth than those with a paper book. However, tellingly, they found no differences in the narrative and descriptive aspects of story recall for stories shared on paper or screen, whether the mother or child was reading. Hence, in contrast to the lab experimental paradigm, where hypotheses that are found to be statistically insignificant are considered to be a failure and often not published, Yuill and Martin's (2016) non-significant findings were very revealing in the naturalistic context—showing how the practice of bedtime reading was not any inferior when reading together from a tablet compared with a paper-based book.

More generally, the study shows how it is possible to conduct a theory-driven experiment in the wild, based on a growing digitalization concern in society, without compromising the experimental design or the control in order to compare conditions. It shows the value of taking into account a wider set of concerns and using a broader set of measures than is usually done in lab experiments. Namely, the *in situ* study provides more ecological validity while demonstrating a wider appreciation of the factors that can influence children's experience of naturalistic shared reading in everyday settings.

Thought Box: A Challenge for HCI Research in the Wild

Instead of having to memorize large amounts of information, most of us simply remember how to find that information using our smartphone. As Dan Chalmers (2008) comments, *"The iPhone has already taken over some of the central functions of my brain. It has replaced part of my memory…It harbors my desires…I use it to calculate, when I need to figure out bills and tips. It is a tremendous resource in an argument, with Google ever present to help settle disputes…I even daydream …calling up words and images when my concentration slips."* To what extent is technology an aid for cognition vs. an extension of the mind? How would you conduct an in the wild study to investigate this?

One way is to select a particular cognitive phenomenon that appears to be changing and run a semi-controlled study in the wild. For example, a project by Linda Henkel (2014) investigated whether photographing objects impacts what is remembered about them. Participants were taken on a guided tour of an art museum and were asked to observe some objects while photograph others. The findings from the study in the museum showed that participants remembered fewer objects that they had photographed and fewer details about them compared with if they had only looked at the objects and not taken a photo of them. This initial finding suggests that people may rely on their camera more to remember rather than attend and process information around them. When asked to pay attention by zooming in on a detail of an object people are able to remember—suggesting that our attentional and cognitive processes are more engaged in focused activities.

2.7   CONCLUSION

Early critiques of cognitive science set a precedent for the need and then later the wider acceptance of doing HCI research in the wild. A number of technologists, designers, and social scientists are now researching a range of topics in the wild: designing and implementing technology interventions, being concerned with the impact of new technologies on behavior, communities, society, and the world at large. While many do not see the need for using or developing theory in HCI, we argue that it can have an important role in RITW. On the one hand, it can inspire and guide the design of technologies and the design of an empirical study. On the other, it can provide an extended or new account of a behavior observed in a naturalistic setting. The challenge is to develop and use theory in the wild that can account for multiple factors and their interdependencies. In the next chapter, we consider the various methodological approaches that have been deployed when conducting research in the wild.

CHAPTER 3

Approaches to Conducting Research in The Wild

3.1 INTRODUCTION

A key concern for RITW is what approach and methods to use. Whereas in lab settings there is an experimental paradigm that sets the parameters and criteria for what is acceptable, within RITW there is not a set methodology to adhere to in the wild. The reason is that there are many different ways to find out how people approach, use, engage, or ignore technology that is placed in or designed for a naturalistic setting. Typically, however, a RITW project involves some kind of a novel technology deployment in an "unconstrained environment" (Brown et al., 2011) and an evaluation of how people respond to the deployed technology. Many RITW projects are set up to trigger a change or elicit a response, such as seeing whether an ambient installation in a workplace would change people's behavior (Hazlewood, et al., 2010; Rogers et al., 2010), determining how people would play a novel mobile game in an urban environment (Benford et al., 2006), and whether groups of tourists would use a group planning application on a tabletop in a tourist information center (Marshall et al., 2011). Various kinds of approaches are adopted for this purpose, including ethnography, participatory design, and research through design (Zimmerman et al., 2007).

The focus of a RITW project is often on how to engage a community so that they can participate in the project and be able to see the value of the technology intervention, adopting, using, and accepting it. As noted at the end of the last chapter, a few researchers have begun conducting experimental studies in naturalistic settings to investigate a specific behavior associated with a technology, such as how people remember now they have smartphones at hand or how reading practices are changing with new types of digital reading devices. Commonly deployed methods include: observations of what people do, using field notes and video; asking people to reflect using diaries and interviews; and logging software and hardware interactions. Here, the focus is on understanding how everyday cognition and living is or might be changing as a result of the uptake of new technologies.

A central concern for many RITW projects is what technologies to design and deploy—given the potential of novel technologies to provoke different behaviors. For example, can a physical display provoke community engagement in ways not possible before? In this chapter, we describe the different approaches and methods that have been employed in research in the wild projects, focusing on those that have been used when deploying, designing, and implementing novel technologies in the wild.

3.2   PARTICIPATORY AND PROVOCATIVE APPROACHES TO RESEARCH IN THE WILD

Two relatively distinct approaches that have been adopted in RITW studies are: participatory and provocative. The first involves *participation* from members of the setting in the design of the technology to be deployed. The approach draws heavily from related perspectives such as action research (Hayes, 2011) and participatory design (e.g., Kensing and Blomberg, 1998)—that emphasize the involvement of end users to create useful systems *per se* (cf. Ehn 2008). Where RITW participatory approaches differ from these is their stronger emphasis on the development of innovative situated technologies and the understanding the context of use. The second provocative approach involves the deployment of technologies that have been developed by research teams, or by artists collaborating with research teams, in order to *provoke* members of a setting to act, react or reflect in various ways.

3.2.1   PARTICIPATORY APPROACHES

A number of participatory approaches have been suggested for creating more sustainability in the wild interventions, including programs to develop technical skills in community members so that they are able to adapt and maintain technologies themselves; using novel configurations of off-the-shelf technologies rather than developing fully bespoke systems (Taylor et al., 2013; Balestrini et al., 2014a) so that the level of expertise required to work with these systems is reduced; and galvanizing participation around an existing community issue (Le Dantec and DiSalvo, 2013) so that the problem of creating engagement is solved prior to deploying the technology. These approaches have aimed for more sustained engagement from communities and appropriation and adaptation of the deployed technologies. However, the opportunity for research teams to develop and test more innovative technology solutions is consequently reduced.

An important but often overlooked consideration when designing with others in the wild is how to manage that process, especially if it is scheduled to take place over several months, involving several stakeholders or user groups. Orchestration becomes key, where a plan, a script, or other coordination mechanism provides an orienting device, a logistical structure, or other support. A number of conceptual frameworks have been proposed to help guide researchers and participants design novel technologies. These range from top-down approaches intended to help researchers create novel experiences to more bottom up frameworks that are developed for members of the general public and local communities to use to coordinate their co-work and design. An example of the former is Benford and Ginannachi's (2011) framework that provides guidance on the design of mixed reality performances based on the approach of "interleaved trajectories" that combine structures of space, time, interfaces, and roles. An example of the latter is Balestrini et al.'s (2017) City Commons framework, which was specifically developed as an accessible and actionable coordinating device to be used by local communities to help them build and deploy their own environmental sensing tools, while helping them produce and manage their own resources. The framework also ended up as a narrative that everyone could share and refer to when talking with others about the project as it evolved over time. In this sense, it acted as a boundary object (Star and Griesemer, 1989), helping to manage the social, political, and technological dynamics that arose.

While working with end users in framing and designing technology offers significant potential for the development of robust systems that are able to be appropriated by members of the setting, and which might sustain use beyond the end of a research study, participatory approaches face a number of challenges. For example, bespoke technologies developed by researchers can break or become obsolete, creating an ongoing need for technical support (Taylor et al., 2013), limiting opportunities for appropriation beyond the end of the project and demanding continued support from members of the research team. Furthermore, issues such as the need for continued funding can stymy projects once research budgets disappear.

3.2.2 PROVOCATIVE APPROACHES

Provocative approaches involve the deployment of technologies that have been developed primarily by research teams—or by artists collaborating with research teams (Benford et al., 2013)—and that have little or no grounding in the existing practices of the setting in which they are deployed. Crabtree (2004) developed the idea that this kind of deployment can be seen as a "breaching experiment." He draws from Garfinkel's (1967) characterization of a research approach that is purposefully disruptive in order to make visible the expectancies that provide the background to everyday social interactions. Crabtree (2004) also argues that a novel technology intervention can be thought of as a breaching experiment, as while it does not necessarily disrupt existing practices it provokes the members of a setting to create new practices to make the technology work in ways that are responsive to its contingencies. He describes three different deployments of a mobile mixed reality game called "Can You See Me Now," describing how participants produced and used a shared body of common knowledge about the local environment and about the variability of GPS coverage to play the game. Understanding of the novel practices that were provoked by each deployment was fed into subsequent technology development, increasing the sophistication of the intervention with each iteration.

A closely related concept is the "technology probe" (Hutchinson et al., 2003), which is a simple, flexible technology that enables practices with and around the technology to emerge that can then inspire future design. Technology probes have three aims: (i) to foreground and understand the perspectives and concerns of participants within particular settings (often the goal is not to develop prototypes that actually fit with these perspectives and concerns); (ii) to field test technology prototypes; and (iii) to inspire both users of the technology and the design team to think about new technologies. An example of a technology probe is the HomeNote device: a situated messaging tool for the home that was developed, deployed, and studied by Sellen et al. (2006). This comprised a fairly simple tablet device that users could send text messages to, which could be annotated by writing on the device. The study identified a range of message types that users sent and highlighted how the success of the device depended on the existing culture of the home and where the display was positioned: both rich contextual factors that could be taken into account in the design of a future home messaging system. Another example of where a technology probe was used to inform the development of a technology was the Physikit toolkit (Houben et al., 2016); a number of households were given a physical toolkit to monitor changes in their home environment, including noise levels, humidity, and CO_2 levels. Their interactions with the physical devices were logged together with collecting other qualitative measures, including their reflections based on diary entries and interviews (this project is presented as a case study in Chapter 4).

In the wild deployments are typically framed in terms of the possibilities presented by new technical developments, such as location technologies (e.g., Benford et al., 2006) or the availability of robust multitouch displays (Marshall et al., 2011). However, as they are primarily conceived and developed by research teams, a potential criticism is that they can be viewed as something done *to* members of a setting rather than done *with* them (Tolmie and Crabtree, 2008), as participants' responses to technologies they have chosen and set up themselves may be different from the ones provided by researchers.

3.3   DESIGN METHODS USED FOR RESEARCH IN THE WILD

A number of methods have been used to design technologies intended for in the wild; many that are commonly employed in user-centered design and participatory design. These include co-design techniques such as sketching, low-tech prototyping, and envisioning. Findings from ethnographic studies and the application of design principles are also commonly used as sources of design inspiration. As deadlines are of the essence, agile programming and UX sprints are increasingly used. Sometimes, bodystorming (Oulasvirta et al., 2003) has been found to be useful when envisioning how a proposed novel technology will be used. By this is typically meant "working the space" (Schleicher et al., 2010); designing and trying out how something will be used in the place it is intended for. For example, when developing the ambient displays in the Clouds and Twinkly Lights installation, intended for an open plan building, the designers walked several paths through the building and imagined where people might pause or sit within the space to locate places for where best to place them, and in doing so imagining how people might notice them as they moved about the building (Hazlewood et al., 2010). They also experimented with sensor pads to determine how they would count the number of people entering and exiting an elevator—including pushing trolleys laden with refreshments (this was found to be a common practice) and walking with different gaits.

Testing evolving designs that are to be placed outdoors can be difficult—especially when considering how the technology will stand up to the elements (e.g., bright sunshine, heat, heavy rain) or when there is no ready supply of electricity or patchy or non existent WiFi signal. The vagaries of heavy-handedness, typically exhibited by boisterous children, can also break or destroy a prototype in a flash. Designing for robustness, therefore, is an important concern. It is also frequently the case that tweaking and debugging has to be done on the fly *in situ* to deal with unexpected obstacles or people not noticing the technology. For example, in one of our tabletop studies (Marshall et al., 2011), members of the design team worked *in situ* observing interactions with the table and adapting the interface, adding online instructions, changing the contrast, adding animation to attract attention, and moving signage to find the place where it could most easily be seen and read.

3.3.1 DESIGNING ON THE FLY DURING RESEARCH IN THE WILD STUDIES

One of the challenges of conducting RITW is dealing with the unknowns and the unexpected. There can be many unforeseen practical issues that need to be dealt with on the fly when conducting RITW. The work to make the project work can sometimes be greater than the development of the technology, itself. In addition, important factors that influence how someone will approach or use a technology placed in a public setting that do not materialize during the design process—may only become apparent when placed in a setting. This is especially the case when it is not be possible to know much about the actual setting before setting up—as happens in a pop-up or temporary place, such as a festival, a hackathon, or a street party. In these contexts, the infrastructure that will house or support the technology only materializes at the event. For example, a physical questionnaire system that was built for gathering feedback in public places, called VoxBox (Gallacher et al., 2015), was only able to be set up and used for the first time outdoors at the event itself—which was a park in London. While an outline plan was provided of where the installation was to be placed in relation to others in the park, it was difficult to envision what it might look like or how it would be approached. Visiting the park beforehand simply showed how vast the space was. It was hard to imagine thousands of people milling around and whether they would approach Voxbox, with so many other stalls that would be erected, vying for their attention.

3.3.2   DESIGNING FOR APPROPRIATION: HOW TO INVITE AND GUIDE THE GENERAL PUBLIC

The findings from many RITW studies have shown how people approaching a novel technology do so quite differently from how researchers expected them to. This is not surprising in settings where the researcher is not at hand to guide or give instructions. Passers-by are left to their own devices to work it out. If the interface is simple—such as a voting box or survey, with only a few buttons to choose from—it can be fairly intuitive for someone to know what to do. It can be more problematic, however, if a new kind of technology has been deployed, that passers-by are not familiar with. While the assumption behind the deployed technology is that it has a new kind of interface, that should encourage new kinds of interactions, people's unfamiliarity with it may paradoxically prevent these from materializing in situ.

This can result in people simply moving on before they have even started using a novel technology. Part of the problem can arise because of the mismatch between how it is used in the lab and how it is approached and interacted with (or not) *in situ*—as was found for the planning group app we developed to be used on a multi-touch tabletop to help groups decide where they wanted to visit in a city (Marshall et al., 2011). The planning app was intended for groups of up to four people to use together (such as a family). It was designed to be graphically pleasing and clearly indicated to each group member that they had to stand on one side of the tabletop to make separate choices of where they wanted to go, before pressing a "finish" button and all coming together on one side to discuss from their choices which to keep and which to discard. The app then created an itinerary that was embedded onto a map. Several groups who were brought to our lab successfully used the shared tool together in the way envisioned, planning a day trip to Cambridge. There was much discussion about the options shown when using the app. The same, however, was not true when we placed the tabletop in a prominent location inside a tourist information center. Many people simply walked passed it, some glanced at it and of those who did, a few then went on to tap on some of the objects appearing on the display. Very few groups used the app to its fullest, i.e., planning a trip, combing the different choices, discussing them, and finally printing off a customized map. If they received immediate feedback from their first input, they would continue exploring the interface; if not they tended to walk away. Most revealing was that groups rarely approached the tabletop at the same time or if they did, they did not separate around the four sides of the tabletop. Instead, typically one of them came to the table by themselves, and then called over to their friends or family to join them, if they found it interesting. The others would look on rather than join in at that point. Even more unexpected was on the odd occasion when strangers tried to use the planning app at the same time—not realizing it was a group tool that had to be used together. This often led to frustration and social discomfort, especially if the one who had been there first noticed the other person/s were now preventing them from completing their plan.

Hence, the findings from a number of RITW studies of initial usage have demonstrated that serendipitous lightweight approaching may not be enough to draw people in to use an application and in the manner it was designed for. While prior lab-based evaluations can provide useful insights about a prototype's usability, different behaviors, especially whether, when, and how people approach a technology and decide to use it differ from when invited to take part in a lab study. Bearing this in mind, how do researchers design a technology that invites and guides the general public through an interaction when using it in public? Even making "what to do" and "where to start" seemingly obvious, such as providing larger than life "start here" buttons and signage, may not work. For example, to help people know where to start answering questions for VoxBox, we placed a huge green flashing button in a prominent place on the front of it. In addition, we added a large wooden arrow pointing down at it, with the words "start here" clearly showing. But, no matter how big and in your face the signage is indicating where to start, some people still don't notice the "right" place. What seems like a trivial design concern—showing someone where to start can be difficult.

It is also the case that people approaching a novel technology bring a history of interacting with other kinds of interfaces. When confronted with a new interface they will draw on this stock of familiar interactions, such as tapping, swiping, or pressing. Sometimes, these work but other times they are inappropriate and the expected feedback does not happen. After a few attempts they may get frustrated or feel stupid and walk away. But as people become more familiar with interacting with new devices (such as smartphones and tablets) and interfaces (such as touch screens, speech, augmented reality) they may feel more confident and comfortable experimenting with a new public technology (such as a tabletop) that has been placed in a public setting, like a library or museum, that has an interface they can recognize and understand how to use. This was most evident with our *in situ* studies where we placed physical interfaces (e.g., Voxbox) in public, where a diversity of people approached them with gusto and were able to provide feedback using the various tangible input devices. This is in sharp contrast to our earlier RITW tabletop study, where many passers-by gave up all too quickly, when their touches on the surface did not result in the interface responding in the way imagined. Once passed the "getting started" threshold, we often observed people feeling completely at ease to the extent they became completely engrossed and 'in the zone' when using the physical installation.

3.4   TECHNOLOGIES DEVELOPED IN THE WILD

Developing technologies does not happen in a vacuum. It builds on, is inspired by developments in, and appropriates existing technical infrastructures, such as software frameworks and APIs and hardware toolkits. Existing infrastructures both inspire and constrain the kinds of technologies that are developed in the wild. Novel technologies that become available often inspire RITW projects (cf. Rogers et al., 2002). For example, our Tourist Planner project was inspired by the possibilities provided by robust multi-touch tabletop computers being brought to the market by Microsoft. This enabled us to build on laboratory studies and design work we had been carrying out to design and deploy a tabletop planning application in the rich sociotechnical setting of a tourist information center and study its use for a month.

Software and hardware toolkits, increased diversity in commercial hardware ,and the increase in availability of networking infrastructures have greatly reduced the breadth and depth of technical expertise and the time required to deploy technologies in the wild. For example, the Arduino and Raspberry Pi platforms, and importantly the online communities that have formed around them, significantly reduce the level of electronics expertise necessary to prototype and deploy sensor-based interactive systems in the wild; tools like Weka (Hall et al., 2009) and Wekinator (Fiebrink, 2011) have opened up the use of machine learning and data mining algorithms to a growing community that includes hobbyists and artists as well as researchers studying technology use in the wild; and OpenCV has made available sophisticated computer vision algorithms including gesture and face recognition to projects that may lack such expertise.

While the growth of technical infrastructure has made the development of technologies to be deployed in the wild more straightforward, there are still many challenges that need to be overcome. Existing technical infrastructures such as power and network usually need to be accessed, or, if un-available, need to be constructed or a workaround developed. Infrastructure is usually thought of as something in the background, that supports activities within a particular setting. However, RITW projects can bring issues around infrastructure to the foreground as something that must be under-stood, explored, and adapted (cf. Star, 1999). For example, the Ambient Wood project (presented as a case study in Chapter 4) deployed a mobile learning experience in a woodland environment with very limited existing infrastructure. This necessitated setting up a wireless network across the environment and using ultrasonic "pingers" to trigger content on mobile devices. This infrastructure development involved working with a number of factors, that would not normally need to be con-sidered by researchers, such as how seasonal changes in foliage might affect signal strength.

Furthermore, the availability of toolkits, APIs and frameworks arguably constrains the kinds of projects developed by researchers, as captured by the aphorism "if all you have is a hammer, ev-erything looks like a nail." However, an advantage of a research in the wild approach is that it tests the assumptions of the research teams both about the needs of members of the research setting, and also about the appropriateness of different technologies. It therefore invites researchers to extend or appropriate existing frameworks and toolkits when they reach the extent of what current tech-nologies can do, adding to the pool of infrastructure available to researchers in the next generation of projects.

RITW projects also frequently require engaging with the social and organizational infra-structures of the setting in which the research is being carried out: issues relating to permissions and access often need to be negotiated with gatekeepers or champions; the health and safety of both the research team and members of the setting need to be considered; and ethics or IRB approval processes can be more challenging to navigate as the unpredictability of wild settings make it more difficult to predict. For example, in our Clouds and Twinkly Lights project, once permission to develop an installation had been given from the heads of departments, members of our design team then worked closely with a health and safety manager, to ensure that part of the installation—which comprised a number of spheres hanging above the heads of people walking through the atrium of a university building—was sufficiently engineered and tested to be left *in situ* for a long period of time (Hazlewood et al., 2010).

3.5   METHODS FOR CONDUCTING *IN SITU* STUDIES IN THE WILD

RITW projects usually involve some kind of study of how existing or novel technologies are used *in situ* or of the setting prior to the deployment of a novel technology. These studies have taken a number of forms and often take a pragmatic approach to the collection and analysis of data. However, a common thread is an attempt to understand how people use either existing technologies or novel technology deployments in settings outside the laboratory.

The majority of in the wild studies have used qualitative and ethnographic methods to investigate the use of novel technologies *in situ*. The strength of these methods is that they enable researchers to explore in detail the impact of the deployed technologies and enable unanticipated phenomena to be documented and explained. Crabtree (2004), for example, adopted an ethnomethodological orientation in attempting to characterize the emergent practices through which social order is created by users of these novel technologies.

Many RITW studies have evaluated technology deployments in public spaces through using video data to understand factors such as how people notice, come to understand how to use, engage with, and interact with others when using various interactive multi-user technologies. These data are typically analyzed through video interaction analysis, enabling researchers to characterize the sequential organization of behavior with these technologies. For example, Peltonen et al. (2008) used video analysis to characterize how the use of a large multitouch display installed in central Helsinki was socially organized.

Qualitative and ethnographic methods are also used in participatory in the wild studies to document the impact of interventions, as well as to try to unpick the factors that influence the use of the technology. For example, Balestrini et al. (2014a) used interviews, participatory observations, and questionnaires to try to understand what factors led to a community sustaining their engagement in a technology deployment developed through an action research approach, and other communities adopting and appropriating the deployment. Akpan et al. (2013) carried out a comparative qualitative study by deploying the same interactive installation in several different settings to try to better understand the roles of spatial and social context in determining whether people would interact with the installation.

Comparative quantitative studies are less common in RITW studies because of the challenges inherent in controlling variables in what are unconstrained settings. However, some researchers have experimented with different interface configurations by installing them in the same setting at different times, typically in public spaces where most passers-by can be assumed to be encountering the deployed technology for the first time. For example, Sahibzada et al. (2017) compared three different public display variants in a tourist information center with respect to their ability to attract attention and elicit interaction from passers-by. A more common approach is to carry out analyses on logged data, often derived from technology probes.

3.5.1   NEW WAYS OF COLLECTING DATA

The availability, affordability, and pervasiveness of new mobile and sensing technologies has made it easier and more feasible for researchers to try out different ways of recording, evaluating, and discovering aspects of people's behavior and situation—that was difficult or impossible before. These include the use of smartphones, wearable cameras, mobile eye tracking, and computer vision techniques to infer behavior and internal states, e.g., facial expressions and emotions. New opportunities have been presented to researchers that have resulted in them conducting HCI research in different ways—this, in turn, has revealed new findings and phenomena (Rogers, 2011).

The development of new infrastructures has also enabled new ways of studying how technologies are used in real world contexts, through the collection and analysis of *in situ* data about technology use. A significant focus has been the development of experience sampling and mobile sensing toolkits, such as Aware (www.awareframework.com), Sensus (github.com/predictive-technology-laboratory/sensus/wiki), and Paco (www.pacoapp.com). Experience sampling is an approach in which participants are asked to fill out short questionnaires (often a single question) as they are carrying out their everyday activities, thus increasing the ecological validity of self-reported data and reducing the time between participants carrying out a behavior of interest to the research team. Experience sampling has a long history, but modern experience sampling tools typically run on smartphones and include elements of mobile sensing (Pejovic et al., 2015). Mobile sensing toolkits utilize the multiple embedded sensors in modern smartphones to gather raw data about user behavior and context and use it to inference user activities—for example, data from sensors such as accelerometers, gyroscopes, magnetometers, and GPS can be used to inference the mode of transport a user is taking. Together, experience sampling and mobile sensing offer researchers powerful tools to understand human behavior in context. For example, Pejovic and Musolesi (2014) developed an interruption management library for Android smartphones by sensing different aspects of users' context, such as activity, time of day, and location, and using experience sampling to provide a ground truth of whether the present moment was a good one to be interrupted with a notification.

A related approach has been to deploy technologies that are augmented with logging functionality. This enables researchers to understand some details of how they are used in the wild. For example, McMillen et al. (2010) deployed a mobile multiplayer game called "Hungry Yoshi" via the Apple App store, enabling them to study aspects of *in situ* use by thousands of players over a prolonged period, and use the logged data to identify users to approach with interview requests. Brown et al. (2013) went even further in developing a collection of data capture technologies to study mobile device use in the wild. These include screen capture, environmental audio recording through the phone microphone, video recording of contextual information using a wearable camera, and remote uploading of logged data. This allows detailed log analysis as well as interaction analysis of situated mobile device use, showing how it is enmeshed within other everyday activities, such as having a conversation or being delayed while taking public transport.

Mobile eye tracking has also become more affordable and usable by researchers to measure eye gaze in situ. Dalton et al. (2015) used a mobile eye tracker to see what people look at during a shopping task in a shopping center. They were able to show using this technology that people look at digital displays, more than would be predicted from previous findings about display blindness (Müller et al., 2009) that was based on observational studies, suggesting that people don't look at them, as they are expecting only to see adverts. However, the potential downside is that people might, unwittingly, look around them more—knowing their attention and gaze is being tracked and measured for a study.

While all of the examples of research tools to study technology use in the wild have been so far for data collection, some have also focused on supporting the replay and analysis of data. The two tools, Replayer (Morrison et al., 2006) and Digital Replay System (Brundell et al., 2008), aim to support ethnographers and analysts in making sense of ubiquitous and mobile computing deployments, where multiple video recordings might be made in parallel on both fixed and mobile cameras, participants are mobile, and multiple sensor streams and system logs may be recorded. They do this by synchronizing the different data sources and representing them together to enable the analyst to repeatedly replay periods of the deployment to try to understand the sequential organization of parallel behaviors through interaction analysis, where log data and other videos provide a context to understand what is happening within one mobile context.

3.6   SUMMARY

There are many different methods for conducting research in the wild; which ones are selected and combined depends on the goal of the project. Typically, a RITW study will use a mix of quantitative and qualitative methods, where possible, to glean subjective, reflective, and aggregated findings over time and space for groups of people. The types of technology that have been designed and deployed also vary from off-the-shelf devices to bespoke installations. One of the main challenges when developing technologies to be deployed in public spaces is how to design them to be noticeable, approachable, and obvious what to do. In the next chapter, we make more concrete, through three in-depth studies, how different methods and approaches have been woven together when designing, creating, framing, and evaluating technologies for novel user experiences.

CHAPTER   4

CHAPTER   4

Case Studies: Designing and Evaluating Technologies for Use in the Wild

4.1   INTRODUCTION

There now exists a large body of RITW studies that have been published since the 1990s that vary in scope, ambition, and scale. The kind of technology intervention and its placement has also been broad, from situating a device in a public place for anyone to use, to providing toolkits for particular groups to appropriate in their own homes. Sometimes, a specific societal problem or behavior is targeted, such as unhealthy living, fitness, or energy conservation, where the goal is to reduce or improve upon current levels, by using technology to nudge, suggest, or encourage a different behavior. Other times, the goal is more open-ended, where the aim is to increase community engagement, democracy, and diversity, for example, by encouraging more people to have a say or get involved in a community project, who wouldn't otherwise (e.g., Koeman et al., 2015).

A diversity of technologies have been designed and used to facilitate the desired outcome, from early mobile devices designed for nurses (e.g., Kjeldskov et al., 2004) to more recent studies of sensor-based monitoring technology to explore people's experiences of moving into smart homes (e.g., Mennicken and Huang, 2012) and smart cities (e.g., Ylipulli et al., 2014). Novel technologies have been developed with a specific purpose in mind—often given a label that defines the context or setting they are being used for or with, e.g., urban informatics, civic technology, community technology, public displays, citizen sensing, and personal informatics. The emphasis here is on supporting a socio-technical infrastructure rather than augmenting or changing a specific user behavior.

Another motivation is to explore how newly emerging technologies can be appropriated for a problematized practice or activity. For example, apps have been developed to run on customized tabletops to help tourists plan a day trip (Marshall et al., 2011) and in museums and aquariums to facilitate public interaction with exhibits (e.g., Hinrichs and Carpendale, 2011). Others have created novel physical prototypes, such as using mixed reality, ubicomp technology, or IoT systems in order to facilitate learning or reflection. Examples include the provision of vibrotactile feedback to help children learn to play the violin (Johnson et al., 2013); multimodal feedback to enable orchestra players to practice together (Johnson et al., 2012); and a customized helmet to collect video and other movement data to help improve skiing performance (Jambon and Meillon, 2009).

To explain what is involved in conducting RITW and what can be achieved, we present three of our own RITW studies below. Having first-hand experience and being in the thick of the RITW, has enabled us to go beyond the text of what has been published in a journal article or conference paper. In doing so, we provide more of the story behind the story, including our reflections on the project's contribution to the field of HCI, the dilemmas faced, and where evident, the impact of the work on subsequent research in HCI. At the end of each case study, we use our RITW framework to highlight relative contributions to different strands of research.

Case Study 1 was selected to exemplify an early research in the wild project, where there was much excitement about the new technologies that were emerging and the opportunities they offered to do something new and different (Rogers et al., 2005). The project was also concerned with how to design new learning experiences that would be appealing, provoke curiosity, and facilitate collaboration. The size of the team working on the project was considerable; the duration of the project ran for about a year, from the inception of the ideas to completing the in the wild studies. Much of what was achieved in this project was through ambitious experimenting in the wild to "make a field trip with a difference." As such, it exemplifies RITW that was very much a step in the dark—much of what was explored was untried, unknown, and uncertain. The case study also demonstrates how advances were made on a number of fronts, in terms of design, engineering, infrastructure, and new understandings about technology-enhanced learning.

Case Study 2 was chosen to illustrate how novel kinds of public displays can be designed to have an impact on a community. In the early 2000s, there was growing interest in how emerging technologies could be deployed to encourage groups, communities, and the general public to change their behavior towards a desired goal, e.g., reducing energy consumption. The focus of the *Clouds* and *Twinkly Lights* project presented here was how ambient displays could be designed to nudge behavior (Hazlewood et al., 2010; Rogers et al., 2010). An assumption was that people would notice them when walking past and, in doing so, be prompted to act on what they had perceived. While there have been a number of innovative art installations developed in this area, few have evaluated their efficacy. The case study provides the insights gained from conducting a longitudinal study to this effect. In doing so, it points out how it is not straightforward teasing out potential causes of observed and logged changes in the data that was collected.

Case Study 3 was chosen to show how it is possible to design novel kinds of physical displays that people can program and use in their own homes in order to understand more about a particular process or dataset—in this case it was environmental data about their own homes. There has been much concern in society about who benefits from "big data"—where corporations and businesses are seen as the main benefactors and the general public as the providers of the data. HCI has begun to investigate how to enable the latter to have more access to meaningful data. The Physikit project

(Houben et al., 2016) was an early foray into how to "open up" data to allow people a way of understanding and making sense of it. In particular, it was concerned with how to enable householders to collect, share, and understand environmental data obtained from their own homes through the use of novel physical visualizations. The case study shows how the researchers went about designing a novel interface to make data more accessible, meaningful, and useable.

4.2   CASE STUDY 1: THE AMBIENT WOOD PROJECT

The Ambient Wood Project was concerned with how to design and evaluate novel learning experiences that could seamfully traverse indoor and outdoor settings (Rogers et al., 2005). In particular, it investigated how new technologies could be designed and implemented to bring together the usually separate activities of field trips and classroom lessons—by literally bringing the classroom into the wild and the wild back into the classroom. Children often find it difficult to make the link between what they observe in the field and what they are taught in the classroom. Based on developmental theory about active learning it was hypothesized that providing contextual information and relevant data *in situ*—when children are problem-solving—could extend how they learn while encouraging more self-initiated discovery. How to couple the "doing" with relevant knowledge/concepts raised a number of research questions. These included what kinds of information to provide, when and where to present it, and how to enable children to interact with it.

4.2.1   BACKGROUND

Since the early 1990s, a number of studies started exploring how mobile technology (e.g., Personal Digital Assistants and digital cameras) could be used to enhance learning when outdoors on field trips. It was assumed that providing children with handheld devices while out in the field, could enhance their learning by allowing them to collect, share, and analyze data at the same time as being able to access information via the Internet (Gay et al., 2001; Grant, 1993; Rogers et al., 2007; Soloway et al., 1999). Core challenges raised when moving learning into the wild included:

1. how to provide a suitable infrastructure outdoors that could augment learning a range of activities;

2. how to operationalize relevant learning theory in this context to support a specific kind of learning;

3. how to design mobile devices that are intuitive to use and require minimum learning before being used in the wild; and

4. how to evaluate the learning that takes place *in situ*.

At the time, ubicomp technology was beginning to be experimented with, including exploring how sensors, mobile devices, and middleware could be developed and used. Part of the excitement surrounding the Ambient Wood project was working out how to harness these new technical capabilities. Simply, providing children with free-range access to the Internet while on a field trip was considered not appropriate, as it could distract them from their ongoing fieldwork activities. Instead, much thought was given to what kinds of contextualized information and data to provide and what kinds of devices to use to present this and how it could be interacted with. A core question was how to enable children to observe, understand, and analyze ecological concepts *in situ* that extended their learning without overwhelming them.

At the time, we were fortunate enough to have obtained a large UK EPSRC research grant (called Equator) that was concerned with investigating innovation between the physical and the digital. A team of computer scientists, engineers, artists and developmental psychologists from five universities in the UK (Sussex, Southampton, Bristol, RCA, and Nottingham) collaborated on a number of strands of research to address the technical, theoretical, and design challenges of developing and delivering contextualized information. Instead of asking children to observe, count, or take photos of various species when in the field, that could be examined later on in the classroom, an assortment of novel technologies were designed to enable them to be able to look up or be provided with relevant concepts and data collected in the field. Below, we describe the project in terms of the four bases of our framework: theory, design, technology, and *in situ* study.

Theory

From a theoretical perspective, the idea of extending and augmenting learning activities *in situ* was inspired by: Jerome Bruner's (1973) work on the importance of discovery learning and autonomous learning; Edith Ackermann's (1991) conceptual framing of learning in terms of a dance between "diving in" and "stepping out"; and Donald Schön's (1984) seminal ideas about coupling the dialectic processes of reflecting and acting. These alternative approaches to accounting for learning differed from the commonly held view at the time, which was, namely, that a learning activity leads to reflection, i.e., as a means to an end. Instead, Bruner, Ackermann, and Schön emphasized *active participation* where reflection and action are viewed as being intertwined. Ackermann (1991), in particular, promoted the idea of cognitive growth in terms of stepping back and forth to reflect momentarily before diving back into an experience.

The Logo programming language was developed very much in this vein, where children give commands to a graphic turtle on a computer screen in order to create and explore mathematical patterns (Resnick and Wilensky, 1997). As part of the learning activity, children were encouraged to envision themselves as a turtle, in order to imagine what it could do. For example, when working out how to draw a circle on the screen using the turtle, most children try to walk in a circle themselves in order to work out how to create a circular shape. In this way, children are able to make use of knowledge of their own bodies to make what is abstract more concrete.

The conceptualization of learning as a dance between doing and thinking was used as the theoretical framing for the design aspects of the Ambient Wood project. In particular, it inspired the design of the novel technologies and associated learning activities.

Design

The project developed a number of novel designs that could encourage and support active learning and participation. A design principle that was adopted for this purpose was to make the "invisible" visible and the "inaudible" audible. However, at the time, no one had really experimented with how digital information could pop up at opportune times to be acted upon by learners. This part of the project, therefore, was very much design research. Different kinds of mobile technologies were created and experimented with in order to alert children and draw their attention to particular aspects of the woodland. Certain kinds of digital content were also triggered, depending on where the children were and what they were doing, when either outdoors or indoors. Some devices were designed to enable the children to collect data, themselves, by using various sensors. Others pinged information at them via handheld or other devices, depending on their location and activity.

A further design principle, that became central to the research, was engendering a sense of suspense: our assumption was that this could encourage active learning throughout by keeping the children guessing and wanting to find out more when making connections between what they were seeing, hearing and collecting. At the same time, we were only too aware of the need to not let the technology dominate the activities or for the children to become too preoccupied with using it.

To achieve our design goals, we experimented with a range of contextualized sounds, images, animations, and textual descriptions, for the following ecological processes and behaviors:

- growing processes (e.g., an animation of bluebells growing and dying over time);

- feeding behaviors (e.g., the sound of a butterfly drinking nectar from a thistle);

- recordings of processes (e.g., light and moisture visualizations);

- locomotion behavior (e.g., a video of a creature moving around in leaf litter); and

- dependencies (e.g., an animation of what would happen if a spider and fungus was introduced to the wooded area).

Some of the digital information was a realistic representation of organisms that the children were unable to see and others were abstractions of processes that were not normally visible or audible.

Technology

The different tools created to deliver the contextualized content and enable the children to collect data were created using a combination of handcrafted and off-the-shelf devices. Most notable were (i) the probe tool and visualizations, (ii) the periscope, and (iii) the ambient horn.

(i) The Probe Tool and Visualizations

A probe tool was developed as a handheld device that could sense and record real time measurements for light and moisture levels (see Figure 4.1). Existing scientific probing tools at the time were very expensive and not suitable for our proposed learning activities. Instead, we created and engineered an affordable and easy-to-use sensing device, that had only two settings, that could be toggled between to measure moisture or light. The probing tool was also connected wirelessly to a Personal Display Assistant (PDA) that presented the sensed data collected in the form of simple real-time visualizations. The sensing and display devices were yoked so that pairs of children had to collaborate with each other when using them. One needed to use the probing device and the other the PDA to make sense of the resulting visualizations. Together, they could then decide what and where next to sense, based on the previous finding. The rationale for designing the devices in this way was inspired by Ackermann's ideas about "diving in" and "stepping out." The goal was that in doing so, reflection and sustained hypothesis generation would be encouraged.

To record and save the data collected and its location, we transmitted them to a database on a server. This was then re-represented as individual data points on a bird's eye view map of the woodland that could be shown on a large display. The purpose of representing the data at this level of abstraction was to enable the children to explore it in an aggregated form so that they could reflect upon what they had measured and seen at a higher level and discuss this with each other when back indoors.

Periodically, the PDA also presented contextualized images of a plant or animal together with a voice-over describing an aspect of its habitat—whenever its presence was detected (e.g., next to a thistle). The aim was to provoke the children into looking around them to see if they noticed anything.

Figure 4.1: (Top left) the probe tool; (top right) two boys looking at the reading; and and (bottom left and right) examples of the light and moisture visualizations.

(ii) The Periscope

The periscope was designed as a novel stand-alone viewing tool (Wilde et al., 2003). It was intended to be an organic-looking artifact that children would stumble across in their exploration of the woodland and be able to work out how to interact with it and what it would do. It was designed to play a set of pre-recorded videos about the habitats in the woodland. Much thought went into its design in terms of aesthetics, affordances and intrigue. It consisted of a hooded flat panel display mounted on an upright stainless steel stem with horizontal handlebars that were used to select content on the screen, which was an assortment of short videos (see Figure 4.2). Instead of watching videos in the classroom and then trying to recall their content when outdoors, the aim was to enable children to watch them while in the woodland, where they could then try to discover the organisms that were being presented in the surrounding woodland immediately afterwards. For example, one of the videos was about the lifecycle of bluebells—which were flowering at the time in the woodland.

Figure 4.2: A group of girls looking at a video being played on the Periscope located in the woodland.

(iii) The Ambient Horn

Hidden speakers were initially placed in the woodland to present pre-recorded sounds that represented plant or animal processes, for example, a butterfly sipping nectar. The sounds were played depending on whether the children walked in the vicinity of various pingers that were strategically placed in the woodland. The rationale for triggering ambient sounds was to provoke children to look around them and reflect on what they had just heard relative to where they were in the woodland. However, none of the children noticed the speakers—the sounds played were literally masked or drowned out by other sounds of the woodland. As an alternative we developed a custom built handheld device, called the ambient horn (see Figure 4.3), that children would carry and hold to their ear when notified of an interesting sound that could be heard in the vicinity (Randell et al., 2004).

Figure 4.3: The ambient horn.

The MUD Infrastructure

There were many technical challenges of providing contextualized information and collecting data in situ. For a starter, there were no convenient power points to plug the devices into or a network to push content to and collect data from the various devices (the project was run before WiFi was available outdoors; and wireless telephone technology such as 3G did not exist). This meant we had to create our own network so that digital representations could be pinged, accessed, and sent around the set of mobile and stationary devices. To this end, an adaptive infrastructure, with its own WiFi system, was implemented in the woodland (Weal et al., 2003). It was built so that it could track the physical movement and presence of children as they walked around the woodland, and that could record and save the various kinds of real-time readings collected through the use of the devices. Sensor technology was placed in the woodland to support location tracking together with pingers that could periodically broadcast a unique identifier, enabling the position of the children when in the woodland to be tracked.

Rather than try to develop a completely new infrastructure, a Multiple User Dungeon (MUD) was adapted to orchestrate the interactions between the physical and digital worlds. The MUD was able to provide an invisible, pervasive orchestrator of the physical world, reacting to, and generating events as appropriate. This appropriation of an existing architecture that was designed originally to support collaborative virtual games, enabled interactions of relevance to the learning activities that occurred in the physical world to be modeled in a virtual world. The system also logged the events that took place during the woodland fieldtrip (e.g., probe readings, audio events played) so that they could be replayed in the makeshift classroom. In addition, a number of laptops were placed in trees to create a wide area network (see Figure 4.4). For power, a car battery was used. It was very much a DIY project that required mastering the outdoors.

Figure 4.4: A laptop placed between branches of a tree to provide an aerial as part of the makeshift infrastructure.

In Situ Study

Learning activities

Children aged 10–12 years old were targeted as the user group. At this age, they are still young enough to find novel augmented experiences fun and engaging but also old enough to learn about them in the way intended. Twenty pairs of children were brought to the woodland (about a 20 km drive from their school) for a morning or afternoon session. They did not know quite what to expect. Such suspense was deliberate, serving to heighten their excitement and curiosity as to what they were expected to do. The instructions were also deliberately open-ended to encourage the children to take more initiative in deciding where to go, what to measure and what data to collect. They were also given walkie-talkies to communicate their findings and observations to a remote facilitator, who sometimes asked them questions about what they were seeing and hearing. This form of remote probing was intended to promote reflection.

The data and information collected, heard, and viewed in the woodland was then re-represented via the bird's eye digital visualization on the public display in the makeshift classroom. A further session was held a week later in a school classroom where the data that had been collected in the woodland was transformed into representations of an ecosystem using physical tokens of the organisms found in particular locations in the woodland. This was intended to help the children think about the habitat distributions and interdependencies experienced in the woodland at a more conceptual level, supporting a too-ing and fro-ing between abstract and concrete reasoning via the interlinking of the physical and digital spaces.

Methodology

To determine whether the new technologies could facilitate the processes of diving in and out, an *in situ* study was conducted. Much thought was given to how to evaluate this kind of learning in the wild, especially which measurements to use. The default pre- and post-test paradigm typically used in educational technology research was considered inappropriate for a whole host of reasons, not least, that it would not be able to measure or reveal what happened during the actual learning processes when children were exploring the woodland and interacting with the new devices. Moreover, ascertaining whether their performance in knowledge tests had improved would not show whether and how the children were using the novel technologies to dive in and step out of the learning activities. Instead, the methods were developed that could assess how children learn to step back, reflect, and dive back when *in situ*.

A practical problem faced by the researchers was how to record the children's learning activities, given that each session involved multiple pairs exploring different areas of the woodland at the same time. It is one thing to put a camera on a tripod in the corner of a classroom and let it run. It is another to work out a "mobile" way of recording multiple people moving around a large area. The method that was adopted was to have a roaming cameraperson follow each pair of children, at a distance, to record their actions and conversations. The children's interactions with the devices were also logged in terms of when and where digital events were triggered and what they did in response to using the devices. As it turned out, the children paid little attention to the camera people's presence, neither playing up to the camera nor appearing inhibited. They appeared far more interested in the unexpected and what the devices provided them with.

The data for each event was logged via the network (i.e., probe readings, images, and sounds that were pushed to the devices) and where possible synched with ongoing conversations and actions that took place at the time. In addition, the conversations that took place with the remote facilitators, via the walkie talkies, were recorded and transcribed. Being able to collect a combination of qualitative and quantitative data was considered important for understanding how children were learning in the mix of outdoors and indoors settings.

Findings

The qualitative data analyzed from the video recordings revealed how often children noticed, suggested, mentioned, and performed various activities when interacting with the devices (Price and Rogers, 2004; Rogers et al., 2004). The quantitative data of the usage of the devices also showed how each device was used, what was recorded, what the children said and noticed while in the woodland. Below, we present some of the highlights from the different analyses.

The probe tool was found to be very effective at promoting collaboration, reflection and hypothesizing about the habitat. This was evidenced by the quantitative data collected showing high levels of probing taking place (often hundreds of probes for each pair *per se*ssion), alongside the hypotheses and reflections that took place before, during, and after each probe. These were taken as indications that the joint activity of probing and reading of the visualizations was successful at provoking sustained exploration. The conversations and subsequent collaborative actions revealed many instances of diving in (probing and reading) and stepping out (talking to each other about what it meant and then based on this suggesting another place to probe that would reveal a different reading). There were also many examples of when they suggested to each other where to go to take the most extreme reading (e.g., the wettest, the darkest). This involved them making and then testing their self-generated hypotheses. The video data also showed that after taking a reading, the pairs of children often suggested to each other another place to go to confirm or disconfirm their hypothesis about what the reading would be there (e.g., a dark spot or bright light).

Evidence of further reflection was observed in the makeshift classroom where the children referred to points on the bird's eye data visualization, using it to remember where they had been when taking each of the probe readings. This form of re-enactment led to much discussion about why something was the case (e.g., lots of light readings in one place). In particular, they compared the different probes they had collected, pointing out what they remembered about different aspects of the woodland. They were also able to predict with high levels of accuracy what each data point represented (e.g., high or low moisture or light).

The periscope was found to facilitate further exploration of the physical environment; the children were observed looking for the organisms that they had seen in the videos (e.g., woodlice under branches). The image/voice-overs that popped up on the PDAs were less successful at triggering reflection. Often the children simply did not notice them—being too engrossed in their on going activity or simply not seeing or hearing them. The Ambient Horn was found to be effective at attracting the children's attention and triggering discussion. For example, after hearing and discovering the sound representing "root uptake" some pairs began talking about factors important for plant growth.

Summary

Taken together, the analyses from the Ambient Wood project were able to demonstrate how novel ubicomp technology could be designed and deployed to extend how children learn in the wild—enabling them to switch between different learning activities and, in doing so, initiate their own inquiries. They also showed how the findings from a RITW project can be generalized in terms of lesson learned, for example, in terms of why constraining how mobile devices are used is an effective way of providing contextual information (Rogers et al., 2007). While it is easy to provide each child with a mobile device to work on their own, making them share devices that are yoked requires pairs of children to have to work together. It is this kind of "forced" collaboration that was found to be a powerful way of engendering the dovetailing of discussion and reflection.

The case study also provided much food for thought for other researchers to consider how to conduct in the wild studies for augmented learning, especially in terms of supporting both *seamless* and *seamful* interactions. Several other researchers, working in the field of education and technology, began investigating how else to provide contextually relevant information in order to facilitate collaborative learning and scientific inquiry (e.g., Hwang et al., 2009; Chen and Hwang, 2012; Kurti et al., 2008; Rogers et al., 2007; Moher, 2008). For example, Tom Moher (2006) designed RoomQuake, where a real classroom was augmented with embedded computers and other instrumentation to enable children to locate the epicenter and magnitude of a series of simulated earthquakes. The researchers designed this set-up with the conceit that the phenomena were occurring directly in the room, as if the room were a scaled-down version of a large geographic region. The seismic events occurred randomly throughout a period of several weeks; the students stopped what they were doing, such as learning French, and using the simulated instrumentation determined the epicenter and magnitude. By bringing the wild into the classroom, high levels of engagement and learning about earthquakes was found to ensue.

In summary, the Ambient Wood RITW project was able to demonstrate how to facilitate children's learning through designing playful and innovative technology devices. Moreover, it was able to inspire other researchers to consider how to design and use novel mobile technology outdoors to engender new ways of learning. It also led to new theorizing about how technology could enhance learning, through constraining interactions using hardware and software design (Yuill and Rogers, 2012). Finally, the Ambient Wood showed how the design of innovative technology was able to bring much joy and excitement into learning. Indeed, 15 years later, some of the children (all now adults) recalled how the day they went to the Ambient Wood was one of their most memorable and long-lasting learning experiences.

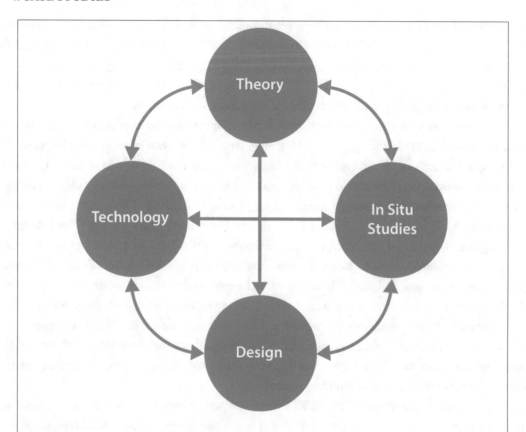

Theory: The project showed how drawing upon theoretical ideas about how children learn through doing could inspire the design of novel technologies that encouraged children to dive in and step out of learning activities, and, in doing so, promote action and reflection. Having one core idea enabled the team to have an anchor from which to develop the technology, design, and *in situ* studies. It also provided the framework for analyzing and interpreting the data collected from the *in situ* studies.

Technology: The project demonstrated how it was possible to develop a range of novel devices, but that this needed to be done in tandem with how they would work with a novel infrastructure that could send and receive information and data.

Design: The project demonstrated how and what kind of contextual information to provide *in situ* that could be accessed through an assortment of handheld devices. It also showed the value of having learning tools that can trigger a sense of wonderment and intrigue.

***In Situ* Study:** The project showed how it is possible to study new learning processes outdoors and indoors through using a combination of qualitative and quantitative methods.

Figure 4.5: Highlights and lessons from the Ambient Wood project using the RITW framework.

4.3   CASE STUDY 2: THE CLOUDS AND TWINKLY LIGHTS PROJECT

The *Clouds* and *Twinkly Lights* project (Hazlewood et al., 2010; Rogers et al., 2010) was developed within the context of the emerging field of ubiquitous computing. The goal of the project was to provide dynamic information about how many people had taken the stairs vs. the elevator during a day and the week through embedding ambient displays in the environment. A specific aim was to determine whether an ambient display could do more than simply inform people; could it also nudge people to change their behavior? In this way, the project combined two areas of research: behavioral change and the design of ambient displays. The idea was to see if people's awareness could be raised through glancing at a display about a particular behavior that they normally overlook or try not to think about and in doing so make them choose an alternative action.

The design rationale was to gently push people towards a desired behavior at the point of decision-making. The behavior of interest was taking the stairs vs. the elevator when moving up and down floors in a building; the desired change was to increase stairs taking. It should be pointed out, however, that there is no right or wrong choice but there are healthier reasons for taking the stairs. There are also reasons why people need to take the elevator, for example, if they have knee or back problems—which has to be dealt with sensitively in the design so as not to exclude or make them feel guilty not being able to participate. Hence, the motivation was not prescriptive but more suggestive.

The setting for the ambient display project was an open plan office building, comprising three floors, at the Open University in the UK (see https://youtu.be/spxlcXTLhdg). The building was originally designed to have many possible ways of walking through it (see Figure 4.6). About 200 people worked in the building at the time of the project, comprising administrative staff, managers, researchers, academic staff, students, cleaners and maintenance engineers. There were also frequent visitors who met with those working in the building or attended meetings, seminars, and other events.

The decision to take the stairs vs. the elevator, when needing to go up or down floors, can happen several times a day for someone working in the building. It was considered important to know why people take one or the other. An initial survey of 30 random people coming out of an elevator of the building was conducted, revealing a number of reasons for taking it up or down two floors, including: because they were unable to walk up stairs due to ill health, were feeling lazy, were carrying things, it was nearer, it was easier, and more certain to find a destination if visiting someone on a given floor. The list of non-essential reasons suggested that it might be possible to nudge people to change their behavior in two ways: at the point of decision-making and through public discussion.

Figure 4.6: The atrium in the building that was chosen for the placement of one of the ambient displays.

4.3.1   BACKGROUND

Mark Weiser's highly influential (1991) paper proposed that the design of future technology should be to make it invisible so as to make it "so embedded, so fitting, so natural, that we use it without even thinking about it" and that they do this by weaving themselves into the fabric of our everyday lives so that they become indistinguishable from it. This vision inspired a generation of researchers to explore how this could be achieved. The field of ubiquitous computing was born. One tranche of research was concerned with designing ambient displays that could be embedded in buildings and public places, that people could glance at to find out something, without being distracted from their everyday lives. Just as someone looks at a street sign and perceives the information conveyed without being conscious they are reading it, so too was it assumed that ambient displays could provide dynamically updated information, that would be of interest to people, such as traffic updates, weather, and stock market prices. The idea was that data could be presented via a physical display, that would change color or shape accordingly; and which could be glanced at momentarily without interrupting someone as they walked passed it.

4.3.2   THEORY

Similar to the Ambient Wood project, theory drawn from the cognitive sciences was used as a source of inspiration when considering what to design. For this purpose, nudging theory was used (Thaler and Sunstein, 2009); it suggests that interventions can be designed to influence and change someone's behavior at the point of decision-making, where they have a choice between A and B. However, it also stresses that nudging is less effective for changing attitudes or patterns of behavior, such as reducing an environmental problem, as it requires making too big a jump from an account of behavior to a desired change in society. Thaler and Sunstein (2009) note how for problems that people cannot solve by themselves, such as reducing pollution, then *"gentle nudges may appear ridiculously inadequate—a bit like an effort to capture a lion with a mousetrap."* (p. 194).

Our idea was to design an intervention that could influence people when making a simple decision as to whether to take the stairs or the elevator when wanting to go up or down floors in a building. In this sense, it seemed like a good candidate for nudging. For this purpose, we considered how to design different kinds of ambient displays that could be easily noticed in a building as people walked passed them. Would people act upon perceiving the changing information in the displays? Furthermore, would they be conscious of changing their behavior in response to noticing the information or would they act without realizing they were being primed?

4.3.3   DESIGN

Suggestions from the theory of nudging about what form the information should take include the type of wording used, the form of labeling, and the positioning of physical signs. However, it does not suggest how to design technology in order to change people's behavior. There are many kinds of ambient displays that could be designed—the question for us was which to choose from? We could use many form factors such as shape, size, color, metaphor, 3D, movement, humor, numbers, and so on to convey the information in different places.

We came up with a number of ideas but they all looked a bit amateur. The research team also had wildly different ideas of what to use, from simply putting numbers on the elevator doors to pointing fingers placed in strategic positions. We all considered it important that an ambient display be designed to fit in to the building and look professional so that people would take it seriously. In the end, we decided to hire a professional to come up with a design concept, and asked Susanna Hertrich, an independent interaction designer, who had much design experience in developing public installations for architectural spaces. After much discussion about the project, she suggested designing a distributed system that could be observed from different viewpoints throughout the building so that everyone entering and exiting the building from different places could notice it. She came up with the concept of three inter-linked displays that could be strategically placed throughout the building. She also stressed the importance of them having an aesthetic and poetic quality. They were called the *Twinkly Lights*, the *Clouds*, and the *History*. The twinkly lights were intended to be placed near the elevators and stairwells, the clouds in the public atrium, and the history display on a large digital screen located near the main entrance to the building.

The *Twinkly Lights* were designed as an abstract representation, that was meant to be playful and attractive, luring people to take the stairs. When someone stepped on the carpet near the stairwell, a moving pattern of pulsating bright lights would be generated. The intention was that the lights would lure them toward the stairs (see Figure 4.7).

Figure 4.7: The *Twinkly Lights* design and actual embedded in the carpet tiles.

The *Clouds* were designed as a large fixed ambient display, where the number of people who have taken the stairs and the elevator would be represented as two moving clouds of colored balls (an orange and a grey cloud) hanging from the ceiling in the atrium (see Figure 4.8). The idea was to attract people to glance at them as they entered the building and walked through the atrium or when walking in the open spaces on each floor. The relative height of the clouds were meant to change in relation to the number of people who took the stairs vs. the elevator: the higher up the orange cloud the more people were using the stairs and the higher up the grey cloud the more people were using the elevator.

Figure 4.8: The *Clouds* ambient display hanging in the atrium.

To test the legibility of the design concept of the clouds before building the installation, initial low-tech prototyping was carried out. A simple 3D model was constructed, consisting of tomatoes and mushrooms hanging from a frame by lengths of fishing line. The cloud of tomatoes could be easily moved up and down through the cloud of mushrooms in a manner similar to that of the concept in the initial design sketch. This model was suspended inside our lab and tested in several different orientations to see how clearly someone could discern the two separate clouds. This involved setting a particular orientation (e.g., tomatoes slightly above mushrooms) and having people walk around the room to achieve perspectives similar to those within the atrium (see Figure 4.9).

Figure 4.9: Low-tech model of the *Clouds* display using tomatoes and mushrooms to explore different orientations.

The *History* display was designed to provide more information in a concrete easy to understand form. For this purpose, a more conventional visualization was designed that used a set of pie charts to depict each day if what the previous ratio of logged total stair/elevator usage was (see Figure 4.10). The same colors of orange and grey were used to represent the stairs and elevator so as to make the connection with the cloud display.

Figure 4.10: The *History* display shown on a digital public screen at the entrance to the building.

4.3.4   TECHNOLOGY

The deployment of an ambient display needs to take into account a number of other factors, besides how well it fits into a building and how noticeable it is. In particular, a number of technical challenges and practical concerns need to be addressed to ensure it is robust, safe, and can keep running over long periods of time. Much envisioning of what-ifs and weighing up of trade-offs were considered. In particular, for this kind of project, we were aware that making decisions early on could have enormous consequences for later on in the design process. It also required us consulting with a range of other experts about what materials to use and how to engineer the physical aspects, e.g., how to build a chassis to scaffold the clouds displays in the atrium—all quite different demands compared with other kinds of HCI research. As well as asking users to provide ideas and feedback on the evolving designs, we needed to seek considerable advice from people as diverse as building operations managers, and health and safety engineers, about the ensuing designs.

To this end, the project adopted an approach that involved the additional processes of bricolage and consultancy. Bricolage refers to making resourceful use of the materials at hand and tinkering with them. At hand refers to both what is lying about in the workshop/lab, and what is available online and in the local hardware store. Potentially, there are thousands of parts and components at hand—the problem is one of deciding which to select and tinker with, bearing in mind many factors including matching the design spec, the cost, durability, scalability, and robustness. For this, "shopping" and "sourcing" skills were considered an integral part of the process.

One of the technical challenges we identified early on was how to track people in order to trigger the twinkly lights at appropriate times and to measure how many people took the stairs or the elevators. The infrastructure that was developed for this had to be adapted to fit in the building in terms of finding power sockets and places to put the sensors. Two types of sensor technologies were initially considered: (i) infrared movement detectors and (ii) pressure mats. The setting for the installation influenced our decision rather than a technical reason. Namely, infrared sensors were rejected because of the problem of mounting them in appropriate locations—there were no conveniently placed walls in the open plan building. Instead, a sensor network was constructed comprising a number of pressure mats, which were placed at the base of the staircases and elevators. The pressure mats were positioned underneath the carpet tiles that were already present—which conveniently protected and hid them from view. Again, this decision was based on what was out there for us to use. Fortuitously, it did not require us to rip up an existing carpet or place any additional protective coverage. To make the pressure mats active, we then had to connect them to sensor hubs and power sockets. Again, we were lucky to discover power sockets in a number of floor cavities located in the floor, which conveniently could also house the sensor hubs.

Throughout the process of implementing the technology in the building we had to get permission and approval from the building's operations managers, as well as the health and safety engineers, without giving the game away to people in the building as to what the project was about. Much time had to be spent with these "official" people explaining the rationale, showing the prototypes, and proving that the strength of the supporting structure was safe.

Initially, it was hoped that a mesh of wireless Sun SPOTs could both record and transmit the data to a central server or display device. In practice, the building had too much concrete and metal for this to work reliably, which, along with an extensive highly powered local network, made the radio transmitters of the Sun SPOTs ineffective. This kind of unforeseen obstacle meant having to rethink the implementation on the fly. Arduino boards with additional Ethernet daughter boards were chosen instead. The building, being new, had a large number of high-speed Ethernet links running in an under-floor network to which the boards could link up to. To work around the possibility of network failure, a design emerged to save the state (number of foot impressions) on the sensor hubs that could transmit these totals to the central server, both regularly and at the moment of activation. The network protocol used was a message-based one—rather than opening a permanent connection to the server over a socket. By saving state on the client and server, they could both be restarted during development and then used immediately.

It was also clear from early testing that it would be impossible to accurately measure the exact number of people walking over a single sensor. People would sometimes stand on the sensors for a prolonged period causing multiple readings to be logged and trolleys pushed through the building by catering, delivery, and cleaning staff also caused multiple readings. On reflection, this was considered to be more of an advantage than a disadvantage: by having a system that counted approximate numbers of people meant we could avoid potential issues related to privacy and sur-veillance. Furthermore, by collecting openly aggregate, anonymous, and approximate information, it was thought that people in the building would not feel they were being forced to use the stairs rather than the elevator. In order to change people's behavior it was considered not necessary to be completely accurate—but just show a change in sensor readings over time.

A matrix of balls was implemented for the cloud display using 24 large fiberglass spheres fixed to a support chassis structure attached to a bridge on the second floor of the atrium. Each sphere was connected to the structure using thin see-through fishing line so as to appear to be float-ing inside the atrium. This part of the work was complex requiring much time and effort. Ensuring the actual installation does what it is supposed to do can often be a big challenge with unforeseen obstacles and complications. Such technical and logistic roadblocks can happen alongside hardware breakdowns, as well as service and admin problems, all of which affect and constrain how much of the initial design idea can be implemented.

Another design consideration was how to introduce the installation in the building without drawing attention to it being a research project. A main motivation behind the project was to dis-cover whether people glance up at the displays. If they had been told in advance, then they would have been primed to look at them in the context of taking part in a research experiment—which is precisely what we did not want to happen. Part of the research was to explore how people discover, appropriate, ignore, and use the displays in situ, without having an experimenter or researcher at hand to tell people how to use something or what it meant. Hence, how and when to introduce the ambient displays was not straightforward. We did not want to send around an email to everyone or place posters up explaining the aim of the project or what the displays were meant to convey, as we felt that could also bias, prejudice or prime people in how they approached the displays. We wanted to see how and whether they were influenced in the manner we assumed ambient displays would work. We decided to deploy the *Clouds* and *Twinkly Lights* displays on a Sunday, when no-one was in the building, so that people would just happen upon them on entering the building on the Monday, when coming to work. We then set up the *History* display one week later, when we had collected data from the pressure pads for the first week.

4.3.5   IN SITU STUDY

Methodology

When conducting an experiment, it is typical to have a control condition to compare findings against. A desirable alternative for an in the wild study is to have a baseline, where data is collected before the proposed intervention. In this project, a six-month study was conducted to obtain a baseline of stair/elevator usage in the building. We were able to gather data for this period of time as it was simply a matter of placing the sensors under the carpet tiles without causing any concern or disruption.

The data was able to provide a representative profile for diverse periods of time (e.g., weekends, holidays, busy days, fire drills, seminar days, special functions, maintenance). The actual study was designed to last for eight weeks. This was considered a sufficiently long period of time to overcome the novelty effect while also see persistent changes in behavior. It also was the deadline for the end of the project in terms of resources, researcher time, and the need to write up the work.

Because the number of people who worked or visited the building each day was in the hundreds it was not possible to track each one precisely each day for weeks on end. For this we would have needed to track the GPS signals on their smartphones. This approach was considered undesirable and unnecessary as it would have meant we could have identified people's movements and working patterns—which was not the purpose of the study. It would have also raised issues relating to privacy—which again was not the purpose of the study. Instead, we used a mix of standard data collection methods: (i) observations of what happened around the displays; (ii) interviews of people while walking through the building *in situ*; (iii) responses to an online survey; and (iv) logged data of stairs and elevator usage. Using such a combination of methods enabled both qualitative and quantitative data to be subsequently analyzed, providing a detailed account of what people did when moving through the building and their views about the displays and stair/elevator usage.

To begin, we observed people moving through the building, by sitting near to the displays or standing by the elevator. We took notes of overheard conversations, observed behaviors, and unusual happenings. We then waited a further two weeks after the displays had been placed in the building before interviewing people. We asked 25 people at random, who were passing through the atrium area, whether they had noticed the displays and, if so, what they thought they meant. We then waited a further two weeks before sending out an online survey that asked a number of questions about people's perceptions of the displays and whether it had impacted them to change their behavior. For this method, we sent out a short web-based survey to mailing lists that covered all the people in the building and to members of a broad-distribution mailing list, which included visitors. To incentivize participation we offered a prize of £100 to the lucky winner. This had the desired effect of over a 70% return rate.

Findings

A problem of having a distributed display throughout the building, so that it could be seen from different entry and exit points, was that it made it difficult to discern what might be affecting people's behavior. If we noticed a change in the data collected for the stairs taken, could we then attribute this to the *Twinkly Lights*, the *Clouds*, the *History* display, or a combination of two or three of them?

From our initial observations, we noted how the occupants of the building were curious about the displays—evidenced by the discussions had among groups of people as they walked passed them. While people on their own glanced at them and carried on walking, whenever a group of two or more came upon the *Twinkly Lights*, they asked each other if they had noticed them or knew anything about them. When subsequently asked in the interviews and online survey, most people answered that they had understood the *Twinkly Lights* to be signaling to them; they should follow them towards the stairwell. In this respect, the *Twinkly Lights* were able to draw people to a point where making a decision could be nudged. In contrast, there were mixed reactions to and accounts of the *Clouds* display. Some people said they did not have a clue what they meant, nor did it concern them, while others worked out that as the displays changed throughout the day, that they correspondingly represented something changing in the building.

However, it proved more difficult to determine from the various findings whether and what level of nudging occurred. On the one hand, most people said it had not affected their behavior, with only a few saying they had changed their behavior in response to seeing the displays (when asked in the survey), while on the other hand, the logged data of footfall showed a statistically significant increase in the proportion of stair usage after the installation. Which was the case?

It is well known from psychological research that there can be a difference between what people say they do and what they actually do. The disparate findings from our *in situ* study indicated this might also be the case. An alternative explanation is that the ambient displays had the effect of increasing awareness about stairs and elevators usage that, in turn, may have unconsciously nudged some people to take the stairs at choice moments—which they may subsequently not have remembered. Examples of choice moments could have been after lunch or when someone was feeling lazy.

Our observations also showed very few people stopping to take a look at the *History* display, and only a few glancing momentarily at it when walking past. This suggests a form of display blindness was at play. For many months, before the study, the public display had been showing slides of research projects and achievements, which had not been updated for a long time. When asked about it, several people said that this kind of display was more informative than the *Clouds*. However, others were adamant that it would not affect their behavior, while some were more philosophical about its value in terms if getting them to think about that they and others do in the building over time. For example, one person made a rather scathing comment about how it showed up the behavior of his fellow workers as "the lazies," who tended to come in mid-week and use the elevators.

Summary

The findings from the *in situ* study did not show a strong effect of the ambient displays on people's behavior over time—indeed, this would have been quite remarkable if it had. Rather, the study showed a small but persistent change in behavior over a long period of time. Because we collected so much data from the sensors, the surveys, the observations, and the interviews, it required us doing detective work; analyzing patterns between and across the different streams of data to ascertain what might be responsible for this. The use of a combination of methods enabled us to explore and tease out possible causes of the differences. Inevitably, there was a lot of "noise" in the data but we were able to conclude that the ambient display intervention had some impact on people's behavior—insofar as there was a reduction in people taking the elevator that persisted over two months.

Compared with a controlled experimental study, we can't say that the findings from our study were able to support the ideas behind nudging theory. However, what we can report is that an ambient display system was able to be deployed and work in the way we hoped, based on ideas derived from both nudging theory and the vision of ubiquitous computing. In so doing, we were able to show how theory can be used in RITW, not to make predictions about behavior, but to generate designs that could influence behavior in a naturalistic setting. Another important finding was to show how human behavior is unpredictable in the wild. People did not seem to know their behavior had changed or when it changed; few people took any notice of the more informative display (the *History* display) while many enjoyed engaging with the *Twinkly Lights* as a form of play. In this respect, it did not matter to us to be able to say with certainty that a particular kind of ambient display was able to nudge people to change their behavior. This way of conceptualizing behavior is in sharp contrast to how researchers try to control it in the lab—where the goal is to show that it is predictable and people respond in the same way when asked to react to a stimuli.

The project also demonstrated how it is possible to scale up a study, in terms of what is gained and what is lost in terms of researcher control. Here, we were able to explore the behavior of several hundred people over several months in the wild. We were able to overcome the novelty effect and demonstrate sustained behavioral change—without researchers needing to be present. Once, when the *Twinkly Lights* had to be removed for maintenance, there were several "complaints" from people working in the building about their disappearance; they had gotten so used to them being part of their daily routine, watching them come on as they walked towards the stairwell. They had, so to speak, become like a pet, as well as part of the furniture.

Figure 4.11 highlights the contributions made to research in the wild using our framework; the size of the circles indicating the relative contributions made for each strand of research.

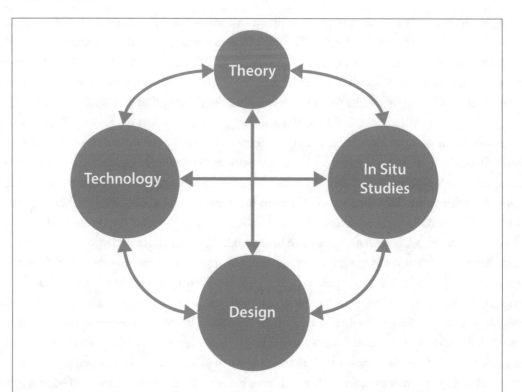

Theory: The study showed how a theory about nudging and a vision about ubiquitous computing could be used to generate the basis for a design concept for an ambient display intended to trigger behavioral change.

Technology: The study showed how it is possible to build an ambitious technical installation but as the team was relatively small, it was important to consult with experts to make it happen. This required getting these people on board and being able to provide evidence to convince them of the value of the project. It also demonstrated how practical and technical challenges can often determine the final design, and hence being adaptable and having a plan B and even a plan C to fall on is important.

Design: The project demonstrated the importance of involving others to ensure it was professional and safe, including talking to a number of experts in different domains and employing a professional designer who had much experience in designing installations for public spaces. It also showed the value of considering aesthetics in the design process and demonstrated the importance of developing an adaptable and flexible methodology that included much bricolage and consultancy throughout.

In Situ **Study**: The project showed how it was possible to install a display without telling people what it was about (ethics clearance was obtained a priori) and only afterward when conducting a survey and interviewing people. This was considered important so as not to prime people into changing their behavior "to help the researchers." The study also showed how it was possible to conduct *in situ* study over several months and the value of having a baseline before implementing the system to determine if and how people changed their behavior in a public building and what patterns could be detected that might be responsible for these. It also demonstrated how collecting different types of quantitative and qualitative data can provide evidence from which to draw conclusions from but not to make strong claims when there are many possible factors at play.

Figure 4.11: Highlights and lessons from the *Twinkly Lights* and *Clouds* project using the RITW framework.

4.4   CASE STUDY 3: THE PHYSIKIT PROJECT

The previous case study demonstrated how it was possible to make advances on three research fronts in terms of technology, design, and an *in situ* study while showing how theory from the behavioral sciences and a vision from computing science were instrumental in shaping these. The third case study, Physikit (Houben et al., 2016), was also inspired by a vision—this time the more recent IoT. More generally, it was concerned with what is happening in society and how technology could be designed to address this. A central concern was how to design more transparent interfaces for IoT technology that could enable the general public to understand and make sense of them.

Compared to the previous two case studies there was not a particular theory that was used to drive the research, rather a desire to provide society with a new way of accessing data. The novel technical intervention involved designing a set of physical cubes that could be programmed to behave in particular ways to alert users to various environmental events (e.g., high humidity). An *in situ* study was conducted to explore how householders approached, appropriated, and used the physical data devices when situated in their own homes. Logged data from how many rules were made and behavioral data were collected from interviews and diary entries.

The contribution of the project to RITW was to show how a novel physical display device could be designed and deployed, that householders could program using simple rules so that they could find out more about their home environment by observing changes to physical displays. It demonstrated the value of providing a new kind of device as a way of enabling the general public access to data that is normally inaccessible or unavailable to them.

4.4.1   BACKGROUND

Recent visions of the IoT have promoted removing users from being in control of systems, to enable greater speed, optimization, and efficiency gains (e.g., Greengard, 2015). Humans are seen as unreliable and expensive in this context. In their place, robots, sensor networks, machine learning, and smart algorithms are being developed at a pace that can sense, detect, alert, action, and maintain a whole range of urban systems, services, and infrastructures. From manufacturing to security, logistics to transportation, and more recently for urban and domestic settings, IoT is finding its place. The goal is for the machines to be able to do the work without the need for humans to check, monitor, and maintain them. Example technologies, such as driverless cars, smart buildings, drones, and domestic robots, are being developed literally to take the control out of the hands of users.

While the push toward ever more interface-less services and apps that run in the background will have many benefits for society, there will be, arguably, many situations where it is desirable for people still to be involved, to understand, be in control, and have the ability to intervene when they want to change settings, when they don't agree with what actions are being selected or when things don't go according to plan. HCI researchers are recognizing the importance of putting the human in the loop and have started to conduct research investigating the human side of data analysis and IoT. Topics of concern include acceptance and appreciation of the data being sensed, the information provided, the actions suggested/taken, ethical concerns especially concerning privacy, trust, acceptance, control, intelligence, avoidance, surveillance, and helplessness. Questions being raised include what do users want to know and how do they discover this.

4.4.2   THEORY

The motivation for the Physikit project was primarily a sense of inequality about who in society benefits from advances in IoT and big data. So far, it has largely been big business and corporations who have gained from having access to it—rather than the general public who tend to provide the data from their shopping habits, online behavior, smartphone usage, etc. The project wanted to begin redressing this imbalance by investigating how new tools could empower the general public more. Compared with the previous two case studies, the research was not theory-driven but more community-driven.

The starting point of this project, therefore, was to develop a technological intervention that could address a societal concern. This form of motivation is increasingly common within research in the wild, where the goal is to problematize and address a particular issue, such as air quality, dampness, and conservation. In this case, the aim was to find a way of making environmental data collected in people's homes (e.g., noise levels, humidity, CO_2 levels) accessible, legible, and actionable. The objective was to make multiple streams of data over time interesting, relevant, and comparable. Inspiration was drawn from physical computing research that investigates how the affordances of physical interfaces can help people understand and make sense of various kinds of data.

A further motivation was based on the outcomes of an earlier study of how householders had used the Smart Citizen toolkit in their own homes, where it was found to be difficult to understand what the urban data visualizations meant (Balestrini et al., 2014b). For example, participants found it hard to make out what a line graph showing NO^2 over time meant in terms of what was happening in their own home. It is one thing to see a line graph with spikes and troughs appearing over time. It is another to know how to interpret this in the context of what is happening in one's home. It was hoped that by providing householders with a new way of thinking about environmental data they would become more interested in it and understand it more in the context it was collected in.

4.4.3   DESIGN

Physikit was designed as a colorful set of physical cubes that people would find aesthetically pleasing and would want to place in their own homes (see Figure 4.12). The cubes could be customized, for example, dressed up in other material, or parts added to them or objects placed on top of them. The idea was to provide people with a sense of ownership.

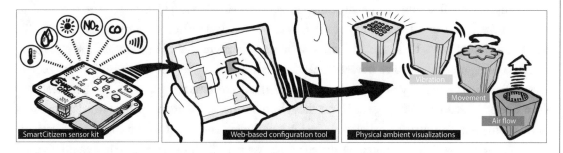

Figure 4.12: Physikit consists of (left) a SmartCitizen sensor kit, (right) four physical ambient visualizations, and (center) a web-based configuration tool to map the sensed data to the cubes.

Much thought went into the design of the form factor, so that the cubes could stand out from a background while also able to be easily distinguished from each other. Another design consideration was that the behaviors the cubes exhibited would be easily noticed and readily understood. A further consideration was what level and amount of visualization to provide. It was decided not to replace the web-based dashboard provided by Smart Citizen's online platform, but to offer an additional way of triggering events that could provide people with a more contextualized entry into theirs and other's data. We were interested in understanding whether this approach was a powerful way of connecting with otherwise abstract "wavy" lines of data being represented over time.

The final designs settled on were: (a) PhysiLight where a LED matrix display embedded in the cube could change color and make different patterns; (b) PhysiBuzz where the cube can be programmed to vibrate at different intensities; (c) PhysiMove where a disk on top of the cube moves clockwise and anticlockwise at different speeds; and (d) PhysiAir that can be programmed to present different air flows (see Figure 4.13).

Figure 4.13: Data is visualized through four cubes: PhysiLight (A), PhysiBuzz (B), PhysiMove (C), or PhysiAir (D).

To set up the behavior of the cubes required a few straightforward steps of "end user programming." A small number of possible mappings and a simple visual language were provided to make up the data rules. Three kinds of rules were provided: (i) when a threshold is reached, (ii) when something is less than, and (iii) when something is more than. For example, the light cube could be configured to visualize how the noise in a house varies over the day: a bright orange pattern indicating it was really noisy while a light green pattern indicating it is quiet. The thresholds were labeled in everyday language as it was thought that this would enable people to relate to them more readily (e.g., country air, exhaled air, inside a chimney) compared with using absolute values.

As well as participants mapping the cubes to events in their own homes, they could also access data from the Smart Citizen kits of other participants. This way, someone could compare their data with their neighbors, to see if they were noisier, or their house was less humid, and so on. The ability to compare one's own data with others has previously been found to be a powerful motivator for understanding and acting on the data shown.

The installation was set up so that participants could choose whether to glance at the changes in the physical displays and make an inference about what they meant, or drill down into the data using the web platform if they wanted to learn more. This two-step design enabled us to explore how much people want to know and are prepared to find out about their data.

Each Physikit had to be handcrafted using a laser cutter, then assembled and tested. The electronics also had to be placed inside each cube, programmed and the various mappings experimented with to make sure they worked. This part of the project proved to be time-consuming and so only a small number of kits were made for the *in situ* study.

4.4.4   TECHNOLOGY

The infrastructure that was used for the project was the Smart Citizen platform (https://smartcitizen.me). This was originally designed to enable people to connect a Smart Citizen hardware-sensing device over WiFi to a web-based platform. The environmental data collected from this device is depicted using a dashboard visualization and accessed via a publically available website (see Figure 4.14). As such, the project piggybacked off an existing infrastructure.

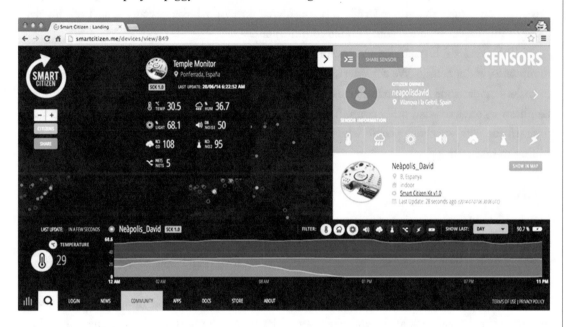

Figure 4.14: A screenshot of the Smart Citizen dashboard, showing time series data and absolute values for environmental data.

A technical challenge was working out how to connect the PhysiCubes to the Smart Citizen API. To this end, a Node.js website was set up to enable data rule management via a web-socket connection. Rules could be created and pushed to a rule engine that could calculate the input-output mapping to control the individual cubes via the web.

4.4.5   IN SITU STUDY

The cubes were initially tested in two of the researcher's homes, to check how they worked when placed in a home setting. This allowed outstanding technical issues to be fixed not foreseen in the lab, e.g., powering the devices in a home, and how to reset the software program without the presence of a researcher. For the actual *in situ* study, a relatively short period of time was planned; one week for the participants to get familiar with the Smart Citizen kit and then a further 10 days where the Physikits were simultaneously deployed in the households. This was considered to be a long enough period to observe sense-making *in situ* and overcome any initial novelty effects while enabling behavior patterns to settle down. While it might have been desirable to run a longer study for several weeks or even months, it was considered unreasonable to expect the participants to give up their time for such a duration. This was because the participants were being asked to write diaries and take part in weekly interviews, in order to collect qualitative data about how they were using Physikit. Any longer than three weeks was considered unreasonable, especially since their involvement in the project required considerable commitment.

The types of households that were recruited were mixed: families with young children, roommates, and a couple. We considered whether to recruit all the same type of participants so as to make comparisons for a particular user group, but this proved difficult to achieve, since many families we contacted had other commitments (e.g., going on vacation) during the proposed study time. In the end, we chose people who were around for the duration of the study and who were willing to take part.

Method

Five households were each given a Smart Citizen Kit that was set up in their homes. They were shown the web platform and how to access their data on it. After the first week, they were each provided with a Physikit and shown how to create rules with it and how to use it with the Smart Citizen toolkit.

During the study, a number of interviews were conducted: at the beginning when setting up, during the study, and then at the end of the study. Participant's interactions using the rule making application and the Smart Citizen data were logged. The participants were also asked to take photos and write a diary about their usage of the Physikit system. The data collected comprised: how many and which mappings participants made between the sensed data and the cubes; the extent to which participants appropriated the cubes when placed in their homes; and how the participants explored and understood the cubes' behavior in relation to the kinds of data being collected.

Findings

The initial part of the study provided a baseline of how many times and what participants looked at when using only the Smart Citizen web platform. It was found that most of the participants stopped looking at their Smart Citizen data after the first two days. Their reasons given during the interviews were that they could not make sense of the data shown on the website in terms of whether it was telling them something good or bad about their homes. After the cubes were installed in their homes, the findings showed them being much more interested in them and for longer. There was also considerable interaction with the cubes and discussion of what their triggered behavior meant.

Participants placed the cubes in communal spaces that were easy to glance at while sitting on the couch when in the living room or sitting at a table when in the kitchen. They also placed them on counters and windowsills—where they would be out of the way but noticeable. Many noted how they were often curious about how their data compared with others—especially their noise levels. Some wanted to know whether they were noisier or quieter than the other householders, and set up the cubes to come on for when they were less or more.

We collected quantitative data about the rules created by the participants by logging their interactions on their tablets. On average, 32 rules were made per household. This was considered to be a large number, indicating sustained curiosity over the duration of the study. As expected, there was a drop-off after initial interest in setting up the rules. The logged data also showed most rules were only maintained for short periods of times before participants settled on one specific rule for each cube. The data collected also revealed the most common mappings made, for example, the cube that had moving parts was connected mostly to the temperature and noise sensors, while the cube with the LED lights was often mapped to the sensed light data.

The findings showed how the participants became more interested in the sensed data over time and what it meant once they began to understand what the events triggered by the cubes meant, be it changes in the configured light patterns, vibration, air, or physical movement. In particular, they became most interested in noise, humidity, temperature, and light levels in their homes relative to others in their neighborhood. Some of the participants started to use the cubes as signals for them to act upon the data. For example, one participant said how they had started opening doors and windows more regularly whenever they noticed a cube indicating the humidity level had risen.

Summary

This RITW project demonstrated how providing householders with an additional physical interface, that was combined with an existing sensing infrastructure, provided them with an interesting way of understanding their own environmental data—that previously they had found difficult to make sense of. In particular, having been involved in configuring the rules and placing the cubes in a particular location, enabled them to more readily make sense of what caused a cube's behavior to change; this in turn guided them to make more sense of the data provided on the Smart Citizen web platform. Often it was the case that a change observed in one of the cubes was enough to inform them, such as the level of humidity had been reached in a kitchen, that they did not feel the need to look at the data on the web platform.

In summary, the project was able to provide a new way of making data accessible to the general public through the use of a physical interface that sat on top of an existing online web platform. This hybrid approach helped people make in-roads into the data, enabling them to work out what was interesting to them. Figure 4.15 highlights the contributions made to research in the wild using our framework; the size of the circles indicating the relative contributions made for each strand of research. As can be seen most of the work focused on designing a system with considerable work developing the technology and then evaluating it *in situ*.

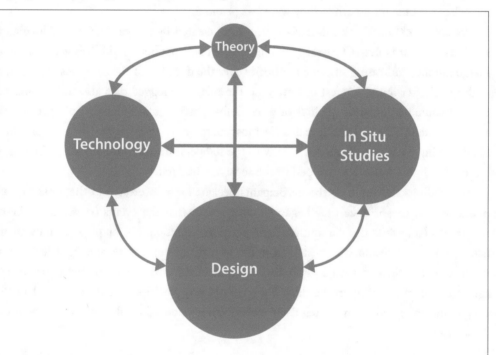

Theory: This project demonstrated how a societal concern could drive the research. As such, there was not a particular theory used but the vision of IoT helped ground the research. The behavior of interest was sense-making of environmental data in situ. However, the project did not use theories of sense-making; rather, it adopted a pragmatic approach to understanding how people make sense of data when provided with a novel technology.

Technology: The project demonstrated the value of designing novel physical displays that mapped onto certain invisible environmental processes. A considerable amount of research was required to create a physical toolkit together with working out how to design an intuitive end user programming interface that householders could use in their own homes with minimal training. Rather than build a completely new database, the project piggybacked off an existing open source environmental sensing system. The technical challenge was concerned with how to achieve this and making the system robust to work without researcher intervention.

Design: The project showed how to develop a distinctive set of attractive and aesthetically pleasing devices that people would be curious about and appropriate in their homes. It also showed how to design a simple end user programming interface for an IoT system—something in itself has been a research challenge within HCI.

***In Situ* Study:** The *in situ* study demonstrated how it is possible to run a relatively short study to obtain a set of findings that showed patterns of behavior beyond a novelty effect. It also demonstrated the value of running a RITW study in two parts, first, to obtain a baseline about how an existing IoT sensing system was used in people's homes and, second, to find out how participants used the physical cubes in conjunction with the IoT sensing system. It also showed the value of using a mixed method approach; collecting quantitative data logged from the sensing system and qualitative data about the participant's experiences, from diaries and interviews.

Figure 4.15: Highlights and lessons from the Physkit project using the RITW framework.

4.5   OVERALL SUMMARY

The three RITW case studies have shown how advances can be made in terms of new designs and technologies, together with discoveries about what happens when situating various kinds of technologies outdoors, in people's homes and workplaces. They have also shown how particular types of theory can help inspire and shape the research, and also how emerging technologies and infrastructures can inspire the design of new user experiences. The summaries depicted in the figures showed how the various strands of research from our framework (i.e., design, theory, technology, and *in situ* study) were addressed in all of the projects but that more emphasis was placed on some (as indicated by the size of the bases), depending on the kind of project.

The case studies have also shown how it is possible to be ambitious, creative, and take risks in terms of experimenting and exploring new areas of research. However, they also highlight how much extra work is needed behind the scenes and the many unforeseen challenges that can materialize. In the next chapter, we discuss these in more detail and other issues concerning the value of RITW given the various obstacles and uncertainties.

CHAPTER 5

Practical and Ethical Issues

5.1 INTRODUCTION

So far, RITW has led by example—through the reporting of case studies and offering up of insights and lessons learned. The outcome of much early RITW has been to open up new research avenues to contemplate what else might be possible. This has enabled the research to be inspired by the possibilities afforded by technology, itself, and for researchers to consider the extent to which it can be designed and deployed in different contexts. It has also opened up new opportunities for rethinking the role of theory in terms of informing the design and framing the analysis. As of yet, there has been little RITW that has fed back into the development of new theory, but that may be just a matter of time.

Clearly, a huge amount of work is involved in RITW; much effort is involved in navigating a range of pragmatic, ethical, and logistical concerns. It is also often expensive, time-consuming, and unpredictable, especially when things don't go according to plan. As the case studies have illustrated, RITW projects often have to deal with a number of challenges and uncertainties. Such challenges are rarely discussed in published studies, and yet the importance of the logistics, the biases that can creep in and the "behind the scenes" work in making research in the wild happen should not be underestimated. Below, we discuss some of the thorny issues RITW has raised in terms of practical and ethical challenges; finishing with a section on the difficulties of publishing RITW given its departure from other kinds of research paradigms within HCI.

5.2 PRACTICAL CHALLENGES

Many practical challenges can arise when conducting HCI research in the wild. Politics also can get in the way of a project's progress, especially if it involves collaborating with other parties. Below we describe four main challenges that can occur.

1. Managing expectations.

2. Identifying and resolving tensions.

3. Dealing with the unexpected.

4. Overcoming the novelty effect.

5.2.1   MANAGING EXPECTATIONS

Project management plays a big part in many RITW projects, especially when overseeing participation, resources and time management. This is most prevalent for large projects, which involve multi-disciplinary teams, where each stakeholder/member is likely to have their own agenda and set of expectations as to how the project will proceed. The process can be helped by adopting an agreed framework, with distinct phases that have a beginning and an end, for example, Balestrini et al's (2017) conceptual framework helped manage the progress of a large citizen sensing project that involved a number of community groups, council officials, volunteers, and researchers.

In the wild studies often raise dilemmas that may be tacit or not a concern in lab studies. For example, Johnson et al. (2012) discuss the role of the researcher and their relationship with participants in RITW, suggesting researchers reflect upon their accountability when running a study, by considering how to manage their influence on their participants. Instead of trying to minimize their effect on participants by distancing themselves, they suggest being up-front about their impact.

However, sometimes it can be awkward for researchers to work out their role within a community. For example, Brereton et al. (2014) found it difficult to undertake ethnographic research and participatory design in a remote part of indigenous Australia for a number of reasons, not least of which it implied unequal power relations between the researchers, themselves, and the Aborigines being studied and whom they wanted to help. The researchers also realized that it was problematic trying to "develop useful designs" based on the outcome of an ethnographic study. Accordingly, they rethought their well-intentioned plan to develop digital noticeboards for the community, based on the outcome of an ethnographic study, as the community did not get what they wanted to do. Accepting their prior assumptions were wrong was both humbling and emancipating. Instead of just observing and codifying what was going on, Brereton et al. (2014) spent much of their time during their visits to this remote part of Australia, developing relationships with the people in the community they encountered. Reciprocity became a focal point where much of their time was taken helping people out in the community, that then led to them sharing and building mutual trust. Part of what they did was very practical, for example, fixing and configuring the community's iPads and setting up Skype for them. They also invited community members to visit their university as part of the reciprocity. In return, the elders, school teachers, and other members of the community joined in more freely with discussions about what they might share using new technology at a forthcoming festival.

5.2.2   IDENTIFYING AND RESOLVING TENSIONS

Tensions may also rear their ugly head throughout a RITW study. A misunderstanding can thwart a project, where partners withdraw because they are unhappy. Planning for such eventualities, however, is not easy since it is difficult to anticipate what might happen. Different stakeholders (e.g., researchers, community members, volunteers) may have different expectations as to what is going to happen and who is responsible for doing what, especially in participatory approaches. For example, tensions arose at various times during Balestrini et al.'s (2017) citizen-sensing project. One tension that was identified was when a decision had to be made when needing to choose between one technology and another for building a prototype system. One group of volunteers wanted to use the Arduino platform while another wanted to use the Raspberry Pi. It was decided to use the latter; however, this left the Arduino volunteers feeling hard done by and some disengaged from the project. A resolution was proposed which was to explore ways in which both could be trialed through a process called "forking" even though it took longer to do so.

Power struggles can also arise with stakeholders who have different agendas. They may feel because they have provided some funding, a venue for the project or access to users that they are entitled to say how the prototype should look and what data to collect. Asking partners to explicate their goals and expectations can help prevent misunderstandings later on in the project when people can be aggrieved that someone else is steering the project in ways not considered desirable.

Concerns about how the impact a project might have on a company's reputation can also affect where an installation can be situated and who can interact with it. For example, Javornik et al. (2017) developed an augmented reality prototype for stepping into character that they wanted to place in the foyer of the English National Opera (ENO) house. The aim of the project was to enable the general public to engage with the installation in order to reflect on what it feels like to be made up as an opera singer. However, a compromise had to be made to place it in a non-public setting due to the high profile of the Opera House; their worry was that such a novel technology might attract potential negative media coverage. To prevent this from happening, it was agreed instead to place the prototype in the principal singer's dressing room and to invite groups of the general public and staff to try it out in this backstage setting.

The researchers also worked closely with a professional Augmented Reality/UX company who provided an existing app for further development for the installation. They, likewise, were very concerned that the final prototype would not be viewed as a gimmick by the public or the press. Understandably, they did not want their reputation to be marred. To overcome this potential problem, much effort went into designing the prototype to have a high level of quality and professionalism.

5.2.3 DEALING WITH THE UNEXPECTED

As we have discussed throughout the book, RITW projects often don't go according to plan. There can be unexpected technical failures, lack of power or WiFi in the vicinity, inclement weather, people not showing up to unlock a building, and so on. Most frustrating is when an authority decides not to give permission to use its premises at the last minute—having provisionally given the go-ahead. Simple and trivial obstacles can get in the way of making it difficult to progress or run a study. Hence, being flexible and agile, and capable of firefighting on the fly, is often needed.

An unexpected problem that can arise is discovering the space is not ideal. This happened when deploying Voxbox in two London parks for a Tour de France bike fan festival. Voxbox was designed as a physical installation to encourage visitors to provide feedback, when answering a variety of questions about themselves (Gallacher et al., 2015). The original idea was that after passers-by had completed answering the questions, they would then go round to the other side of Voxbox to look at the visualizations that they had just contributed to with their answers. A gazebo canopy was erected to protect VoxBox from the sunlight and rain. The organizers of the festival, however, let the researchers know that the public would not be able to enter the gazebo from the back or the sides because of a security risk, meaning that the area behind Voxbox was cordoned off to the public. Hence, to get to the other side of Voxbox meant people having to walk into the covered gazebo from the front. However, the impression it gave was that the general public was not allowed to enter. A workaround, therefore, had to be developed, on the fly, to encourage and legitimize a path for the general public to be able to come through the front into the enclosed area (see Figure 5.1a). While far from ideal, a blackboard was also placed outside the entrance with big arrows painted on the floor it directing people to come inside. Some people did come in but not nearly as many as those who came to look in front of the gazebo.

A week later, Voxbox was set up at a second Tour de France event held in another park in London. The pitch provided in this setting was quite different—a corner (see Figure 5.1b), meaning that VoxBox could this time be positioned at an angle that allowed people to move freely around both sides. Compared to the first setting, many more people were observed milling around the two sides.

Hence, a seemingly small, physical constraint, based on unexpected logistics sprung upon the researchers by the organizers, can have a big impact on the way the general public perceived, approached, and decided whether to commit, participate, and complete a set of actions the technology was designed for. This was difficult to foresee, despite months of working with the event organizers, including getting approval for health and safety, doing a risk assessment, measuring the space and planning where power would come from and the hiring of the gazebo to enable entry from all four sides.

The general public can also be very unpredictable when interacting with a new installation they come across, especially children. Watching children interact with some of our prototypes when placed in a museum or a public viewing space has shown how violent they can become, slamming buttons, pulling parts off an installation with great force, and kicking them. This kind of boisterous behavior can destroy a well-crafted interface in a matter or seconds. When we saw this happening to one of our prototypes in the entrance of a museum in Germany we asked for it to be moved to a supervised room further back in the museum. This had the desired effect of reducing the impact of high-spirited and disorderly conduct.

Figure 5.1: The two different locations where VoxBox was placed at the Tour de France Fan Park: (A) one closed off at the front with a small entrance and (B) the other at a corner, allowing people to move freely between either side.

People can also start interacting with a prototype in ways unintended. This is especially the case for one-off-use contexts, such as museums and shopping malls, where the expectation is for brief walk-up-and-use explorations. People vary in what they notice and try out when encountering technology in situ. For example, our study investigating how a software tool running on a new tabletop technology in a tourist information center could facilitate group planning, revealed how our envisioned use rarely happened. Families and groups of friends did not come to the tabletop all together and use it as a group. In fact, it was used very differently to the ways we had observed groups of participants using it in the lab. The difference was quite striking. Whereas in a typical lab study, participants are brought in and shown their place by a researcher and given instructions on what to do, such guidance is largely absent in the wild. Rather than see this as a failure of our design we saw it as a lesson learned about how groups rarely come together to an installation and understand that they have to take their place to simultaneously to complete a task.

5.2.4   OVERCOMING THE NOVELTY EFFECT

There is an emerging expectation that an in the wild study should be sufficiently long enough to overcome the novelty effect. By the novelty effect is meant the special interest and initial effort people make to use a technology because it is new to them. For example, people spend much time using a newly procured device, such as a smartwatch or a home assistant. The first few hours/days typically show a high level of interest that then usually subsides. If people continue to use it over a sustained period of time, then it can be said to have overcome the novelty effect. Of interest is how they adopt, appropriate, and use it in their everyday routines once the novelty effect has worn offs.

However, determining what is acceptable as sustained use over a period of time is highly variable—it could be days, weeks, months, or years. Conversely, some technology interventions are deliberately designed for one-off encounters, such as exhibits or installations situated in shopping malls, museums and high streets. In these contexts, the novelty effect is actually what is of interest. Do members of the public notice it and if so, do they stop, approach it and interact with it? Repeat visits may provide additional information about their use, but it is the way passers-by initially engage with them that is important.

A growing area of RITW is concerned with charting patterns of longer use, such as how people change their eating habits or exercise regime, after being provided with a wearable activity tracking device. In this context, analyzing how people use a device in the first few days would give only a snapshot view of its effectiveness. In contrast, analyzing patterns of usage over weeks and months can demonstrate whether the device has a lasting effect on someone's attitude and/or behavior. It is usual to see an increase or decrease in a desired activity, followed by a drop-off after a few weeks or sometimes months. It might also show that, even though people may no longer use the device, it has had the desired effect of increasing their awareness. For example, Clawson (2016) and Harrison et al. (2015)investigated the growing concern that personal health tracking technologies are failing to inspire long-term adoption. Clawson used an unusual method of analyzing the sale of second-hand wearable devices via classified ads online sites, such as Craigslist, as a way of trying to understand the sellers' reasons for wanting to get rid of the technology. By analyzing the wording used in the ads, they were able to show that people stopped using their wearable devices for a range of reasons, including buying an upgrade, reaching their goals, and a mismatch between what the device could do and what they expected it to do. Moreover, they were able to demonstrate that simply stopping using a device does not mean it has failed. In fact, they found that 10% of the ads were posted because the owners wanted or had bought the latest model, while others stopped using them because of a change in their personal circumstances, such as having a baby.

5.3   ETHICS: CONSENT, DATA COLLECTION, AND PERMISSION

Conducting RITW raises a number of ethical concerns especially when the research is concerned with what the general public will do without being told what to do. For example, when placing technology in public places for passers-by to use, it can be problematic informing them in advance about the project and have them explicitly consent to participate. Walking up to someone and handing them an informed consent form is likely to make them suspicious and they may try to avoid you; as if trying to sell them something or doing some market research. Instead, a common practice is to put up a poster (cf. Heath et al., 2010) nearby that provides information about the research project, what data is being captured, such as video, and what participants can do if they object to data about them being captured (we usually provide pictures of those members of the research team who may be in the vicinity as well as contact details and make it clear that data will be immediately deleted on request). In some countries, however, it is more challenging to run a RITW study in public because of privacy laws.

The intention is that members of the public can discover for themselves the motivation behind the technology and what is expected and therefore choose whether to participate. However, people may not notice the posters and if they do, may not bother to read them, before moving on. This might be seen in some HCI circles as an ethical dilemma, since it is expected that researchers ask people, taking part in a user study to read and sign a consent form; partly, to let them know that they can withdraw at any point from the study, if they feel uncomfortable, for whatever reason. In particular, the consent form is meant to provide participants with reassurance about what they have let themselves in for; it tells them their "rights" when taking part. Ethical guidelines such as those provided by the British Psychological Society (2010) typically suggest limiting observation without explicit consent to public spaces where people would normally expect to be observed anyway. When conducting research in the wild, it is important that designers consider supporting people in choosing whether to voluntarily approach and engage with a novel research technology, knowing they can step away at any time.

Paradoxically, there may be less pressure on passers-by to complete an activity than there is in a lab study, precisely because they have not signed a consent form. There isn't usually any visible pressure or demand characteristics in the wild, that can sometimes be implicit in a controlled study and which can influence how participants cmplete a set of tasks. Furthermore, as noted in Case Study 2 (where various ambient displays were deployed to nudge people to take the stairs more), having informed the building occupants about the purpose of the study *a priori* would have most likely biased the results.

Deciding how best to capture what people do in naturalistic settings can also be problematic. It is often desirable to capture as much as possible, using video or audio recording, so as to analyze it in more detail later. However, some members of the public may object to being filmed in a public setting without their consent. Likewise, householders may not want cameras in the privacy of their own homes. Management of a public space may also say no because of company rules about security. For example, trying to video in a shopping mall or airport is often a no-no because of the owner's concerns about security risks. In some of our projects, we have not been able to obtain permission to film and have instead made notes when observing from afar. It can also be difficult to work out whom to ask to get permission—if it is a publicly owned place, such as a park or a street, where many stakeholders may have a vested interest in the space.

Even when given permission to film in a public place, there is still the problem of knowing what to do if a passer-by does not want to be videoed. If the researcher is present, they can intervene and delete that part of the video. But when a study is running for several weeks or months, it may not be possible for a researcher to be at hand all the time to watch out for this. Providing information about how the video data will be used and stored can help but it may not be reassuring to the public.

Researchers like to find out as much as they can. However, walking up to someone who has glanced at a public display but has then decided not to interact with it—to ask them why they didn't participate—is likely to be uncomfortable for both the researcher and the passer-by. It can easily result in defensive behavior on behalf of the passer-by as it puts the onus on them to explain their non-behavior. It is much easier and more comfortable interviewing people after they have participated than those who have not. And yet, it would be really valuable to know why they chose not to take part.

In situ studies where participants are provided with a technology to use in settings such as their own homes, schools, or workplaces are different. Here, an agreement is often set up between the researcher and the participants, and as part of this process informed consent is typically granted at the start. However, the process is much more complicated when participants use a research technology, but have not had direct contact with a member of the research team. This is becoming increasingly common in mobile application deployments through app stores. In these situations, it is far from clear whether participants consent, or even realize that they are participating in a research project, particularly where that information is contained in the terms and conditions pages for the app as these are often not read (Morrison et al., 2014). To address this dilemma, researchers are beginning to develop sets of ethical guidelines for app deployments (McMillan et al., 2013).

There are still many issues to resolve in considering ethics in RITW projects. In particular, there are many uncertainties and ambiguities associated with implementing ethical protocols. For example, it is impossible to fully predict how people will use the technology (indeed, this is one of the main reasons for conducting in the wild studies in the first place!), and therefore ethical issues may emerge through the analysis of research data (Rooksby et al., 2016). A number of researchers have argued for the need to move away from a view of ethics as a bureaucratic step that should be completed prior to research getting under way (cf. Brown et al., 2016), to something that is "in action" (Frauenberger, et al., 2017) or "situational" (Munteanu et al., 2015), meaning that use of the technology cannot be fully anticipated prior to the research getting under way and, therefore, consideration of ethics requires the attention and agency of the research team to work through emergent issues as they arise.

Another dilemma facing researchers working in the wild is what role they take after having introduced themselves to a particular participating group, who have agreed to take part, when in their home, school, or work place. In this context, do researchers account for and manage their influence on participants in the wild and when to ask questions from them? While this is something that ethnographers have to manage when observing and asking members about their work or other practice it can be awkward when conducting an in the wild study of a deployed technology where the researcher does not want to influence the outcome. Rose Johnson discussed this dilemma at length when spending a week at a summer school aimed at violin players practicing for a concert (Johnson et al., 2012). She approached the violin players who agreed to try out her augmented haptic feedback technology that she had designed to help them practice and play together. She needed to show them how to use it and set it up (it was a wearable technology that needed calibrating) and also observe them using it during practice sessions. As she was an amateur violin player herself, she decided to be a paying participant at the summer school, as well as taking on the role of researcher/observer. This allowed her to empathize and understand what it was like for them to practice with and without the wearable haptic device. Had she chosen to take the role of just being an observer/researcher, who introduces the technology and observes their practice, she would not have been able to gain the insights she did, as it would have been much more difficult to be aware of what was happening around her. At first, the participants were happy to try her technological device for certain sessions and share their experiences of doing so with her. As the week wore on, she began to feel tired and suffered a lot of pain in her back and shoulders, from bad posture and playing for too long. After taking some painkillers when sitting down at one session, she noticed how the others also had packets of painkillers next to them. They, too, appeared to be suffering from pain. This made her anxious as to whether to continue asking them to use the haptic devices during practice sessions (which they had previously found to be helpful) and also if and when it was appropriate to ask them questions about it—given they were in pain. In the end, they were able to share their various pains with her, and this empathy enabled them to let her know when not to ask them about their experiences of using the prototype.

5.4   PUBLISHING RESEARCH IN THE WILD

Finally, we consider the dilemma of trying to publish in the wild research since it does not follow or adhere to the same scientific criteria of rigor associated with lab studies. We have had several of our papers rejected because the reviewers note that there wasn't a control to compare our *in situ* findings with. Sometimes, it is possible to overcome this objection by establishing a baseline of what people did before the intervention and then observe and measure behavior afterward—as we did for the *Clouds* and *Twinkly Lights* and Physikit projects. However, even then, it can be difficult to ascertain whether it is the novelty of the intervention that is contributing to changes in observed behavior. It could also be caused by changes in other factors such as time of day, the weather, etc.

When things don't go according to plan in the wild, for example, communities don't reduce their energy consumption as hoped or people don't take part in community events as envisioned, it has been known to make this the focal narrative of a case study. For example, Gaver et al. (2009) published one of their RITW projects that unraveled in terms of design failures, citing the many reasons why their novel sensor-based system—intended to promote reflection from homeowners about the well-being of their home—were unsuccessful. These included problems inherent in the mappings they used between the data collected and the way it was represented in the prototype and problems with the design processes they used. These kinds of salutary "lessons learned" approaches demonstrate how reporting failures can be equally as important as reporting success stories of technology deployment studies.

Another problem that can arise is how to recognize the various contributions of a team of researchers working on the same research in the wild project. The fear of "salami-slicing" or "double-dipping" can mean that a large body of work—sometimes a year or more's worth of work, involving several researchers, ends up only being reported in one article. For the Ambient Wood project we were able to publish the various strands of research in different specialized venues, for example in design, educational and technical conferences, enabling the respective researchers to be first author on at least one paper. Since many RITW projects involve a number of researchers it is important to decide who will be the lead author early on in the project and then for subsequent publications, so as not to disappoint or make someone feel it is unfair—especially in view of the meritocracy researchers are typically appraised against.

CHAPTER 6

Conclusions

One of the questions often asked of research in the wild is how does it differ from other approaches, such as action research, ethnography, participatory design, and Research through Design, or technology probes? We have argued throughout the book that RITW does not set itself apart from these—rather it sees them, similarly, as being in the wild. What RITW emphasizes is how to provide a different framing and way of pursuing research that strives for ecological validity, especially in the context of a history of HCI that has been dominated by controlled lab-based experiments, lacking ecological validity. Similar moves are starting to happen in psychology, where the ecological validity and generalizability of lab experiments are being called into question. It is important to recognize that this sea change has come about partly through new technologies enabling new methods to be used. For example, smartphones are now being used in psychological science research as the equipment for presenting materials over indefinite periods of time and also for recording a range of behaviors, for example, language learning, memory, stress levels, emotions, and body language. In lab settings, psychologists have to design their experiments to fit in with relatively short time frames (typically an hour) to accommodate participant visits. This problem is obviated when conducting research in the wild; accordingly, the experimental design can be varied a great deal more, both temporally and spatially. Arguably, the data collected in more naturalistic settings is more akin to how people think, reason, feel and learn in their everyday lives, and hence can open up whole new paradigms by which to study how people learn, remember, forget, get anxious, and so on in their own lives. However, it should also be recognized that there are still likely to be many reasons for continuing to conduct research in controlled lab settings, especially when it involves testing new interfaces and interaction techniques intended to help people to develop skills for new application areas, such as learning to fly.

So what next for RITW? How will the landscape of HCI change over the next few years? What new contributions will be made and new directions taken? Is RITW here to stay or will it be overtaken by the next turn in HCI? Will there be a call to return research to the lab—a call for rigor? Clearly, there are many situations where running an experiment is cheaper, easier and can provide the control to be able to test how people's responses and reactions to stimuli—where it is not so important to determine how people will approach, notice, or use something in a naturalistic setting. Measuring task completion time and errors will still play a major role in a range of user studies, as mentioned above, where understanding how performance is affected is paramount.

However, it is without question that RITW is growing and making new contributions—in terms of advancing theory, designing new experiences, implementing novel technologies *in situ*, and discovering how people behave, embrace, or react against digitalization, in all its manifestations. Indeed, there is a growing concern within HCI and beyond, about the impact technology is having on society, for example, how people are becoming ever more hyper-dependent and hyper-connected (Harper et al., 2008): overwhelmed by email, over-exposed by Facebook, addicted to perpetual digital checking, unable to read deeply (Carr, 2011), and so on. With every new hype and worry surfacing about technology, HCI researchers are now considering it their responsibility to investigate such claims (Rogers, 2011).

It is not surprising, therefore, to see a call for arms for HCI to address societal concerns, by alleviating or improving upon them, through designing and investigating new technology interventions. Topics that are being mooted are far-reaching, including climate change; health and well-being; facilitating innovation in developing countries; and instrumenting new forms of transportation and connectedness in urban living. Such societal questions, however, need the HCI community, along with others, to change how research is done. They require scaling up and at times, compromising how research gets done, involving new framings, new collaborations, and new integrated methods (Shneiderman, 2016).

But where to begin? How can researchers help to make the world a safer and more peaceful place (Hourcade et al., 2012); to save the planet through more sustainable everyday and working practices (Di Salvo et al., 2010); to enable developing countries to be empowered to design and build their own technologies (Rogers and Marsden, 2013)? Will a RITW agenda lend itself to addressing these? Such lofty ambitions require RITW to scale up, with different framings, methodologies, and collaborations with others. Such an enterprise will inevitably require a number of departures from the way RITW is currently conducted. However, its experience with scoping research in terms of a broader context suggests it can provide a starting point from which to expand its reach—considering larger-scale problems that traverse temporal and geographical boundaries.

Shneiderman (2011) suggests addressing societal concerns in terms of macro-HCI (in contrast to micro-level research that was traditionally done in the lab). This requires thinking at a different level of granularity as to what to design and how to evaluate it. This will involve exploring a range of topics (e.g., trust, privacy, safety, pro-social behavior) in the wild at a more coarse-grained level. Alternative values, new measures, and different dialogs will be required to make sense of this new wild landscape. As part of this broader scoping, there needs to be a debate about what constitutes HCI research vs. what is an extension/adaptation of volunteering/charity or other work—and if so, does it matter.

For innovative solutions to be successfully developed there needs to be greater involvement and integration across a number of disciplines and communities (Jurmu et al., 2016). A challenge will be working out how to team up with others in order to conduct scaled-up research in the wild. Collaboration can be very hard to achieve and manage—especially when there are novel combinations of researchers from different backgrounds (e.g., architecture, machine learning, education), others working in applied professions (e.g., transport, retail, healthcare, sport) and the general public at stake. Inevitably, compromises will need to be made, when trying to push for making both a research contribution and a societal impact. Tensions, misunderstandings, and politics will also erupt in unexpected ways. RITW will need to innovate not only in what it focuses on but also how it works with others.

There are also many opportunities for new kinds of research to emerge that not only can address larger societal issues, but also provide new methods for investigating how people use, adopt, and rely on technology in wildly different contexts. For example, technology is beginning to be developed that provides hybrid experimental methods—that can be used safely in naturalistic settings, where it might be considered unethical or too dangerous to test a new technology in the wild. Previously, HCI researchers have used simulators to provide a safe environment to see how people drive, react and problem-solve under different real-world conditions. In the future, it may be possible to develop new kinds of experimental methods that are more affordable and allow for real world testing. For example, Wang et al. (2017) recently developed a novel method for studying how drivers behave in future autonomous driving scenarios when driving in a diversity of real world conditions. Their system, Marionette, uses a Wizard-of-Oz protocol that transmits steering wheel motion from a real steering wheel (controlled by an experimenter) to the simulated wheel but without providing actual control. The participants driving the car know this to be the case but the Wizard-of-Oz set-up allows them to suspend their disbelief when driving the car. Using their adapted Wizard-of-Oz method, the researchers were able to set up a series of research experiments in authentic driving conditions, on the Stanford University campus. They investigated how participants sitting in the driver's seat reacted to conditions where the autonomous system was behaving unusually, and which required an emergency hand-off back to them to take over. They found considerable variability in how people react, with some people taking over immediately and others being much more hesitant, taking considerable time before taking back the control.

There will also be new opportunities for using technology in innovative ways to understand the effects of digitalization on society—how technology across the spectrum is being adapted and appropriated. The availability, affordability and pervasiveness of new mobile and sensing technologies is making it easier and possible for researchers to no longer need to be experts in programming or engineering, but to be able to try out different ways of recording, evaluating, and understanding a diversity of behaviors situated in real-world contexts—that was difficult or impossible before. These include the use of smartphone apps, wearable cameras, mobile eye tracking, open APIs, and computer vision techniques to infer behavior and internal states, e.g., facial expressions and emotions.

Finally, as well as providing greater ecological validity, RITW will enable the next generation of researchers to begin theorizing more ecologically about cognition in the world. It is exciting times for those concerned with understanding the complex relationships between human behavior and technology, for example, in terms of cognitive development (e.g., how we perceive, learn, and remember) and social development (e.g., how we make and keep friends, how we conduct conversations). We end by asking how will researchers change what they do in the light of seeing more?

References

Edith K. Ackermann. 1991. From de-contextualized to situated knowledge: Revisiting Piaget's water-level experiment constructionism. In Harel, I. and Papert, S. (Eds). *Part 4: Cybernetics and Constructionism*. Norwood, NJ: Ablex Publishing Corporation. 367–379. 36

Anne Adams, Tim Coughlan, John Lea, Yvonne Rogers, Sarah Davies, and Trevor Collins. 2011. Designing interconnected distributed resources for collaborative inquiry based science education. In *Proceedings of the 11th Annual International ACM/IEEE Joint Conference on Digital Libraries (JCDL '11)*. ACM, New York. 395–396. DOI: 10.1145/1998076.1998152.

Imeh Akpan, Paul Marshall, Jon Bird, and Daniel Harrison. 2013. Exploring the effects of space and place on engagement with an interactive installation. In *Proceedings of the SIGCHI Conference on Human Factors in Computing Systems (CHI '13)*. ACM, New York. 2213–2222. DOI: 10.1145/2470654.2481306. 29

Mara Balestrini, Jon Bird, Paul Marshall, Alberto Zaro, and Yvonne Rogers. 2014a. Understanding sustained community engagement: a case study in heritage preservation in rural argentina. In *Proceedings of the SIGCHI Conference on Human Factors in Computing Systems (CHI '14)*. ACM, New York. 2675–2684. DOI: 10.1145/2556288.2557323. 22, 29

Mara Balestrini, Paul Marshall, and Tomas Diez. 2014b. Beyond boundaries: the home as city infrastructure for smart citizens. In *Proceedings of the 2014 ACM International Joint Conference on Pervasive and Ubiquitous Computing*. ACM, 2014. 987–990. DOI: 10.1145/2638728.2641557. 61

Mara Balestrini, Yvonne Rogers, Carolyn Hassan, JaviCreus, Martha King, and Paul Marshall. 2017. A city in common: A framework to orchestrate large-scale citizen engagement around urban issues. In *Proceedings of CHI 2017*. DOI: 10.1145/3025453.3025915. ACM. 7, 23, 71

Steve Benford, Andy Crabtree, Martin Flintham, Adam Drozd, Rob Anastasi, Mark Paxton, Nick Tandavanitj, Matt Adams, and Ju Row-Farr. 2006. Can you see me now? *ACM Transactions on Computer-Human Interactions*. 13, 1 (2006), 100–133. DOI: 10.1145/1143518.1143522. 21, 24

Steve Benford and Gabriella Giannachi. 2011. *Performing Mixed Reality*. MIT Press. 22

Steve Benford, Chris Greenhalgh, Andy Crabtree, Martin Flintham, Brendan Walker, Joe Marshall, Boriana Koleva, Stefan Rennick Egglestone, Gabriella Giannachi, Matt Adams, Nick Tandavanitj, and Ju Row Farr. 2013. Performance-led research in the wild. *ACM Transactions on Computer-Human Interactions*. 20 (3) Article 14 (2013), 22 pages. DOI: 10.1145/2491500.2491502. 23

Ofer Bergman and Steve Whittaker. 2016. *The Science of Managing Our Digital Stuff*. MIT Press. 17

Jon Bird, Paul Marshall, and Yvonne Rogers. 2009. Low-fi skin vision: a case study in rapid prototyping a sensory substitution system. In *Proceedings of the 23rd British HCI Group Annual Conference on People and Computers: Celebrating People and Technology* (BCS-HCI '09). British Computer Society, Swindon, UK, 55–64. 16

Jon Bird and Yvonne Rogers. 2010. The pulse of Tidy Street: Measuring and publicly displaying domestic electricity consumption. In *Workshop on Energy Awareness and Conservation through Pervasive Applications, Pervasive* 2010. 1

Margot Brereton, Paul Roe, Ronald Schroeter, and Anita Lee Hong. 2014. Beyond ethnography: engagement and reciprocity as foundations for design research out here. In *Proceedings of the SIGCHI Conference on Human Factors in Computing Systems (CHI '14)*. ACM, New York. 1183–1186. DOI: 10.1145/2556288.2557374. 70

British Psychological Society. 2010. Code of Human Research Ethics. http://www.bps.org.uk/sites/default/files/documents/code_of_human_research_ethics.pdf. 75

Barry Brown, Stuart Reeves, and Scott Sherwood. 2011. Into the wild: challenges and opportunities for field trial methods. In *Proceedings of the SIGCHI Conference on Human Factors in Computing Systems (CHI '11)*. ACM, New York. 1657–1666. DOI: 10.1145/1978942.1979185. 4, 21

Barry Brown, Moira McGregor, and Eric Laurier. 2013. iPhone in vivo: Video analysis of mobile device use. In *Proceedings of the SIGCHI Conference on Human Factors in Computing Systems (CHI '13)*. ACM, New York. 1031–1040. DOI: 10.1145/2470654.2466132. 31

Barry Brown, Alexandra Weilenmann, Donald McMillan, and Airi Lampinen. 2016. Five Provocations for Ethical HCI Research. In *Proceedings of the 2016 CHI Conference on Human Factors in Computing Systems*, ACM, New York. 852–863. DOI: 10.1145/2858036.2858313. 77

Patrick Brundell, Paul Tennent, Chris Greenhalgh, Dawn Knight, Andy Crabtree, Claire O'Malley, Shaaron Ainsworth, David Clarke, Ronald Carter, and Svenja Adolphs. 2008. Digital Replay System (DRS)—a tool for interaction analysis. In *4th International e-Social Science Conference*, 2008. 31

Jerome Bruner. 1973. *The Relevance of Education*. New York: Norton. 36

Graham Button. 2008. Against distributed cognition. *Theory, Culture and Society*, 25 (2), 87–104. DOI: 10.1177/0263276407086792. 17

Jessica L. Cappadonna, Margot Brereton, David M. Watson, and Paul Roe. 2016. Calls from the Wild: Engaging Citizen Scientist with Animal Sounds. In *Proceedings of the 2016 ACM Conference Companion Publication on Designing Interactive Systems (DIS '16 Companion)*. ACM, New York. 157–160. DOI: 10.1145/2908805.2909413. 1

Nicolas Carr. 2011. *How the Internet is Changing the Way We Think, Read and Remember*. W.W Norton and Company. 80

David Chalmers. 2008. Forward. In *Andy Clark Supersizing the Mind: Embodiment, Action, and Cognitive Extension*. MIT Press. 19

Chia-Chen Chen and Tien-Chi Huang. 2012. Learning in a u-Museum: Developing a context-aware ubiquitous learning environment. *Computers & Education*, 59(3), 873–883. DOI: 10.1016/j.compedu.2012.04.003. 45

Andy Clark and David J. Chalmers. 1998. The extended mind. *Analysis*, 58 (1) 7–19. DOI: 10.1093/analys/58.1.7. 15

Darrin Clawson. 2016. How mobile, wearables, iot, and cloud technologies are impacting business every day! *Journal of Computing Sciences in Colleges*. 31 (5), 118–119. 74

Sunny Consolvo, David W. McDonald, Tammy Toscos, Mike Y. Chen, Jon Froehlich, Beverly L. Harrison, Predrag V. Klasnja, Anthony LaMarca, Louis LeGrand, Ryan Libby, Ian E. Smith, and James A. Landay. 2008. Activity sensing in the wild: a field trial of ubifit garden. In *Proceedings of the 2008 CHI Conference on Human Factors in Computing Systems*, ACM, New York. 1797–1806. DOI: 10.1145/1357054.1357335. 1

Tim Coughlan, Trevor D. Collins, Anne Adams, Yvonne Rogers, Pablo A. Haya, and Estefanía Martín. 2012. The conceptual framing, design and evaluation of device ecologies for collaborative activities. *International Journal of Human-Computer Studies*. 70 (10), 765–779, DOI: 10.1016/j.ijhcs.2012.05.008. 8

Andy Crabtree. 2004. Design in the absence of practice: breaching experiments. In *Proceedings of the 5th Conference on Designing Interactive Systems: Processes, Practices, Methods, and Techniques (DIS '04)*. ACM, New York. 59–68. DOI: 10.1145/1013115.1013125. 23, 29

Andy Crabtree, Alex Chamberlain, Matt Davies, K. Glover, Stuart Reeves, Tom Rodden, Peter Tolmie, and Matt Jones. 2013a. Doing innovation in the wild. In *Proceedings of the Biannual Conference of the Italian Chapter of SIGCHI (CHItaly '13)*. ACM, New York. Article 25, 9 pages. DOI: 10.1145/2499149.2499150. 1

Andy Crabtree, Alex Chamberlain, Rebecca Grinter, Matt Jones, Tom Rodden, and Yvonne Rogers. 2013b. Introduction to the special issue of "The Turn to The Wild." *ACM Transactions on Computer-Human Interaction (TOCHI)*, 20 (3), 13–15. DOI: 10.1145/2491500.2491501. 1

Torbjørn S. Dahl and Maged N. Kamel Boulos. 2014. Robots in health and social care: A complementary technology to home care and telehealthcare? *Robotics*, 3, 1–21. DOI: 10.3390/robotics3010001. 1

Nicholas S. Dalton, Emily Collins, and Paul Marshall. 2015. Display blindness?: Looking again at the visibility of situated displays using eye-tracking. In *Proceedings of the 33rd Annual ACM Conference on Human Factors in Computing Systems (CHI '15)*. ACM, New York. 3889–3898. DOI: 10.1145/2702123.2702150. 31

Christopher A. Le Dantec and Carl DiSalvo. 2013. Infrastructuring and the formation of publics in participatory design. *Social Studies of Science*, 43 (2), 241–264. DOI: 10.1177/0306312712471581. 22

Carl DiSalvo, Phoebe Sengers, and Hrönn Brynjarsdóttir. 2010. Mapping the landscape of sustainable HCI. In *Proceedings of the SIGCHI Conference on Human Factors in Computing Systems (CHI '10)*. ACM, New York. 1975–1984. DOI: 10.1145/1753326.1753625. 80

Paul Dourish. 2001. *Where the Action Is*. MIT Press. 12, 15

Pelle Ehn. 2008. Participation in design things. In *Proceedings of the Tenth Anniversary Conference on Participatory Design 2008 (PDC '08)*. Indiana University, Indianapolis, IN. 92–101. 22

Rebecca Fiebrink. 2011. Real-time human interaction with supervised learning algorithms for music composition and performance. Ph.D. thesis, Princeton University, Princeton, NJ, January 2011. 28

Christopher Frauenberger, Marjo Rauhala and Geraldine Fitzpatrick. 2017. In action ethics. *Interacting with Computers*, 29 (2), 220–236. DOI:10.1093/iwc/iww024. 77

Dom Furniss and Ann Blandford. 2006. Understanding emergency medical dispatch in terms of distributed cognition: a case study, *Ergonomics*, 49 (12–13), 1174–1203. DOI: 10.1080/00140130600612663. 17

Sarah Gallacher, Connie Golsteijn, Lorna Wall, Lisa Koeman, Sami Andberg, Licia Capra, and Yvonne Rogers. 2015. Getting quizzical about physical: observing experiences with a tangible questionnaire. In *Proceedings of the 2015 ACM International Joint Conference on Pervasive and Ubiquitous Computing (UbiComp'15)*. ACM, New York. 263–273. DOI: 10.1145/2750858.2807529. 4, 25, 72

Harold Garfinkel. 1967. *Studies in Ethnomethodology (Social & Political Theory)*. Prentice-Hall. 23

William Gaver, John Bowers, Tobie Kerridge, Andy Boucher, and Nadine Jarvis. 2009. Anatomy of a failure: how we knew when our design went wrong, and what we learned from it. In *Proceedings of the SIGCHI Conference on Human Factors in Computing Systems (CHI '09)*. ACM, New York, 2213–2222. DOI: 10.1145/1518701.1519040. 78

William Gaver, Andy Boucher, Nadine Jarvis, David Cameron, Mark Hauenstein, Sarah Pennington, John Bowers, James Pike, Robin Beitra, and Liliana Ovalle. 2016. The Datacatcher: Batch deployment and documentation of 130 location-aware, mobile devices that put sociopolitically-relevant big data in people's hands: Polyphonic interpretation at scale. In *Proceedings of the 2016 CHI Conference on Human Factors in Computing Systems (CHI '16)*. ACM, New York. 1597–1607. DOI: 10.1145/2858036.2858472. 7

Geraldine Gay, Robert Reiger, and T. Bennington. 2001. Using mobile computing to enhance field study. In N. Miyake, R. Hall, and T. Koschmann (Eds.), *Carrying the Conversation Forward*. Mahwah, NJ: Erlbaum. 507–528. 35

Connie Golsteijn, Sarah Gallacher, Lisa Koeman, Lorna Wall, Sami Andberg, Yvonne Rogers, and Licia Capra. 2015. VoxBox: A tangible machine that gathers opinions from the public at events. In *Proceedings of the Ninth International Conference on Tangible, Embedded, and Embodied Interaction (TEI '15)*. ACM, New York. 201–208. DOI: 10.1145/2677199.2680588.

Wayne C. Grant. 1993. Wireless Coyote: A computer-supported field trip. *Communications of the ACM*, 36 (2), 57–59. DOI: 10.1145/155049.155062. 35

Samuel Greengard. 2015. *The Internet of Things*. MIT Press. 60

Mark Hall, Eibe Frank, Geoffrey Holmes, Bernhard Pfahringer, Peter Reutemann, and Ian H. Witten. 2009. The WEKA data mining software: an update. *SIGKDD Explorations Newsletter*. 11 (1), 10-18. DOI: 10.1145/1656274.1656278. 28

Christine Halverson. 2002. Activity theory and distributed cognition: Or what does CSCW need to DO with theories? *Computer Supported Cooperative Work*, 11(1-2), 243–267. DOI: 10.1023/A:1015298005381. 17

Richard Harper, Tom Rodden, Yvonne Rogers, and Abigail Sellen. 2008. *Being Human: Human Computer Interaction in 2020*. Microsoft. 80

Daniel Harrison, Paul Marshall, Nadia Bianchi-Berthouze, and Jon Bird. 2015. Activity tracking: barriers, workarounds and customisation. In *Proceedings of the 2015 ACM International Joint Conference on Pervasive and Ubiquitous Computing* (UbiComp '15). ACM, New York, 617–621. DOI: 10.1145/2750858.2805832. 74

Gillian R. Hayes. 2011. The relationship of action research to human-computer interaction. *ACM Transactions on Computer-Human Interactions.* 18 (3), Article 15, 20 pages. DOI: 10.1145/1993060.1993065. 22

William Hazlewood, Nick Dalton, Paul Marshall, Yvonne Rogers, and Susanna Hertrich. 2010. Bricolage and consultation: a case study to inform the development of large-scale prototypes for HCI research. In *Proceedings of Designing Interactive Systems (DIS '10).* 21, 25, 29, 34, 47

Christian Heath, Jon Hindmarsh, and Paul Luff. 2010. *Video in Qualitative Research.* Sage. 78

Linda A. Henkel. 2014. Point-and-shoot memories: The influence of taking photos on memory for a museum tour. *Psychological Science.* 25 (2), 396–402. DOI: 10.1177/0956797613504438. 19

Uta Hinrichs and Sheelagh Carpendale. 2011. Gestures in the wild: studying multi-touch gesture sequences on interactive tabletop exhibits. In *Proceedings of the SIGCHI Conference on Human Factors in Computing Systems (CHI '11).* ACM, New York. 3023–3032. DOI: 10.1145/1978942.1979391. 33

James Hollan, Edwin Hutchins, and David Kirsh. 2000. Distributed cognition: toward a new foundation for human-computer interaction research. *ACM Transactions on Computer-Human Interactions,* 7 (2), 174–196. DOI: 10.1145/353485.353487. 17

Eva Hornecker and Emma Nicol. 2012. What do lab-based user studies tell us about in-the-wild behavior?: insights from a study of museum interactives. In *Proceedings of the Designing Interactive Systems Conference (DIS '12).* ACM, New York. 358–367. DOI: 10.1145/2317956.2318010. 4, 7

Steven Houben, Connie Golsteijn, Sarah Gallacher, Rose Johnson, Saskia Bakker, Nicolai Marquardt, Licia Capra, and Yvonne Rogers. 2016. Physikit: Data engagement through physical ambient visualizations in the home. In *Proceedings of the 2016 CHI Conference on Human Factors in Computing Systems (CHI '16).* ACM, New York. 1608–1619. DOI: 10.1145/2858036.2858059. 24, 34, 59

Juan Pablo Hourcade, Natasha E. Bullock-Rest, Lahiru Jayatilaka, and Lisa P. Nathan. 2012. HCI for peace: beyond tie dye. *Interactions,* 19 (5), 40–47. DOI: 10.1145/2334184.2334195. 80

Ed Hutchins. 1995. *Cognition in the Wild.* MIT Press. x, 11, 14

Hilary Hutchinson, Wendy Mackay, Bo Westerlund, Benjamin B. Bederson, Allison Druin, Catherine Plaisant, Michel Beaudouin-Lafon, Stéphane Conversy, Helen Heiko Hansen Evans, Nicolas Roussel, and Björn Eiderbäck. 2003. Technology probes: inspiring design for and with families. In *Proceedings of the SIGCHI Conference on Human Factors in Computing Systems (CHI '03)*. ACM, New York. 17–24. DOI: 10.1145/642611.642616. 23

Gwo-Jen Hwang, Tzu-ChiYang, Chin-Chung Tsai, and Stephen J. H. Yang. (2009) A context-aware ubiquitous learning environment for conducting complex science experiments. *Computers & Education*, 53 (2), 402–413. DOI: 10.1016/j.compedu.2009.02.016. 45

Francis Jambon and Brigitte Meillon. 2009. User experience evaluation in the wild. In *CHI '09 Extended Abstracts on Human Factors in Computing Systems (CHI EA '09)*. ACM, New York. 4069–4074. DOI: 10.1145/1520340.1520619. 34

Ana Javornik, Yvonne Rogers, Delia Gander, and Ana Moutinho. 2017. MagicFace: Stepping into Character through an Augmented Reality Mirror. To appear in *Proceedings of the SIGCHI Conference on Human Factors in Computing Systems (CHI '17)*. ACM, New York. DOI: 10.1145/3025453.3025722. 71

Rose Johnson, Yvonne Rogers, Janet van der Linden, and Nadia Bianchi-Berthouze. 2012. Being in the thick of in-the-wild studies: the challenges and insights of researcher participation. In *Proceedings of the SIGCHI Conference on Human Factors in Computing Systems (CHI '12)*. ACM, New York. 1135–1144. DOI: 10.1145/2207676.2208561. 1, 34, 70, 77

Rose Johnson, Nadia Bianchi-Berthouze, Yvonne Rogers, and Janet van der Linden. 2013. Embracing calibration in body sensing: using self-tweaking to enhance ownership and performance. In *Proceedings of the 2013 ACM International Joint Conference on Pervasive and Ubiquitous Computing (UbiComp '13)*. ACM, New York. 811–820. DOI: 10.1145/2493432.2493457. 33

Marko Jurmu, Leena Ventä-Olkkonen, Arto Lanamäki, Hannu Kukka, Netta Iivari, and Kari Kuutti. 2016. Emergent practice as a methodological lens for public displays in-the-wild. In *Proceedings of the 5th ACM International Symposium on Pervasive Displays (PerDis '16)*. ACM, New York. 124–131. DOI: 10.1145/2914920.2915007. 80

Finn Kensing and Jeanette Blomberg. 1998. Participatory design: Issues and concerns. *Computer Supported Cooperative Work*, 7, 167–185. DOI: 10.1023/A:1008689307411. 22

David Kirsh. 2013. Embodied cognition and the magical future of interaction design. *ACM Transactions on Computer-Human Interactions*. 20 (1), Article 3, 30 pages. DOI: 10.1145/2442106.2442109. 16

David Kirsh. 2014. The importance of chance and interactivity in creativity. *Pragmatics & Cognition*, 22 (1), 5–26. DOI: 10.1075/pc.22.1.01kir. 16

Jesper Kjeldskov, Mikael B. Skov, Benedikte S. Als, and Rune T. Høegh. 2004. Is it worth the hassle? Exploring the added value of evaluating the usability of context-aware mobile systems in the field. In *Proceedings of Mobile HCI'04*. Springer, 61–73. DOI: 10.1007/978-3-540-28637-0_6. 3, 33

Jesper Kjeldskov and Mikael B. Skov. 2014. Was it worth the hassle?: ten years of mobile HCI research discussions on lab and field evaluations. In *Proceedings of the 16th International Conference on Human-Computer Interaction with Mobile Devices & Services (MobileHCI '14)*. ACM, New York. 43–52. DOI: 10.1145/2628363.2628398. 3

Lisa Koeman, Vaiva Kalnikaité, and Yvonne Rogers. 2015. "Everyone is talking about it!": A distributed approach to urban voting technology and visualisations. In *Proceedings of the 33rd Annual ACM Conference on Human Factors in Computing Systems (CHI '15)*. ACM, New York. 3127–3136. DOI: 10.1145/2702123.2702263. 33

Arianit Kurti, Daniel Spikol, and Marcelo Milrad. 2008. Bridging outdoors and indoors educational activities in schools with the support of mobile and positioning technologies. *International Journal of Mobile Learning and Organisation*, 2 (2), 166–186. DOI: 10.1504/IJMLO.2008.019767. 45

Jean Lave. 1988. *Cognition in Practice*. Cambridge University Press. x, 11, 13

Zhicheng Liu, Nancy Nersessian, and John Stasko. 2008. Distributed cognition as a theoretical framework for information visualization. *IEEE Transactions on Visualization and Computer Graphics*, 14 (6), 1173–1180. 17

Paul Marshall, Richard Morris, Yvonne Rogers, Stefan Kreitmayer, and Matt Davies. 2011. Rethinking 'multi-user': an in-the-wild study of how groups approach a walk-up-and-use tabletop interface. In *Proceedings of the SIGCHI Conference on Human Factors in Computing Systems (CHI '11)*. ACM, New York. 3033–3042. DOI: 10.1145/1978942.1979392. 4, 7, 21, 24, 25, 26, 33

Paul Marshall, Alissa Antle, Elise Van Den Hoven, and Yvonne Rogers. 2013. Introduction to the special issue on the theory and practice of embodied interaction in HCI and interaction design. *ACM Transactions on Computer-Human Interaction*, 20 (1), 3 pages. DOI: 10.1145/2442106.2442107. 15

John McCarthy and Peter Wright. 2004. *Technology as Experience*. MIT Press. 15

Donald McMillan, Alistair Morrison, Owain Brown, Malcolm Hall, and Matthew Chalmers. 2010. Further into the wild: Running worldwide trials of mobile systems. In P. Floréen, A. Krüger., and M. Spasojevic (eds) *Pervasive Computing. Pervasive 2010. Lecture Notes in Computer Science*, vol. 6030. Springer, Berlin, Heidelberg. DOI: 10.1007/978-3-642-12654-3_13. 31

Donald McMillan, Alistair Morrison, and Matthew Chalmers. 2013. Categorised ethical guidelines for large scale mobile HCI. In *Proceedings of the SIGCHI Conference on Human Factors in Computing Systems (CHI '13)*. ACM, New York. 1853–1862. DOI: 10.1145/2470654.2466245. 77

Sarah Mennicken and Elaine M. Huang. 2012. Hacking the natural habitat: an in-the-wild study of smart homes, their development, and the people who live in them. In *Proceedings of the 10th International Conference on Pervasive Computing (Pervasive'12)*, Judy Kay, Paul Lukowicz, Hideyuki Tokuda, Patrick Olivier, and Antonio Krüger (Eds.). Springer-Verlag, Berlin, Heidelberg, 143–160. DOI: 10.1007/978-3-642-31205-2_10. 33

Pranav Mistry and Pattie Maes. 2009. SixthSense: A wearable gestural interface. In *Proceedings of SIGGRAPH Asia 2009*, Sketch. Yokohama, Japan. DOI: 10.1145/1667146.1667160. 16

Tom Moher. 2006. Embedded phenomena: supporting science learning with classroom-sized distributed simulations. In *Proceedings of the SIGCHI Conference on Human Factors in Computing Systems (CHI '06)*, Rebecca Grinter, Thomas Rodden, Paul Aoki, Ed Cutrell, Robin Jeffries, and Gary Olson (Eds.). ACM, New York. 691–700. DOI: 10.1145/1124772.1124875. 45

Tom Moher. 2008. Learning and participation in a persistent whole-classroom seismology simulation. In *Proceedings of the 8th International Conference on International Conference for the Learning Sciences—Volume 2 (ICLS'08)*, International Society of the Learning Sciences 82–90. 45

Alistair Morrison, Peter Tennent, and Matthew Chalmers. 2006. Coordinated visualisation of video and system log data. In *Proceedings of Coordinated and Multiple Views in Exploratory Visualization*. IEEE, 91–102. DOI: 10.1109/CMV.2006.5. 31

Alistair Morrison, Donald McMillan, and Matthew Chalmers. 2014. Improving consent in large scale mobile HCI through personalised representations of data. In *Proceedings of the 8th Nordic Conference on Human-Computer Interaction: Fun, Fast, Foundational (NordiCHI '14)*. ACM, New York. 471–480. DOI: 10.1145/2639189.2639239. 77

Jörg Müller, Dennis Wilmsmann, Juliane Exeler, Markus Buzeck, Albrecht Schmidt, Tim Jay, and Antonio Krüger. 2009. Display blindness: The effect of expectations on attention towards digital signage. In *Proceedings of the 7th International Conference on Pervasive Computing (Pervasive '09)*, Hideyuki Tokuda, Michael Beigl, Adrian Friday, A. J. Brush, and Yoshito Tobe (Eds.). Springer-Verlag, Berlin, Heidelberg, 1–8. DOI: 10.1007/978-3-642-01516-8_1. 31

Cosmin Munteanu, Heather Molyneaux, Wendy Moncur, Mario Romero, Susan O'Donnell, and John Vines. 2015. Situational ethics: Re-thinking approaches to formal ethics requirements for human-computer interaction. In *Proceedings of the 33rd Annual ACM Conference on Human Factors in Computing Systems (CHI '15)*. ACM, New York. 105–114. DOI: 10.1145/2702123.2702481. 77

Alva Nöe. 2004. *Action in Perception*. MIT Press. 15

Alva Noë. 2009. *Out of our Heads*. Macmillan Publishers. 16

Antti Oulasvirta, Esko Kurvinen, and Tomi Kankainen. 2003. Understanding contexts by being there: case studies in bodystorming. *Personal and Ubiquitous Computing*, 7, 125–134. DOI:10.1007/s00779-003-0238-7. 24

Veljko Pejovic and Mirco Musolesi. 2014. InterruptMe: designing intelligent prompting mechanisms for pervasive applications. In *Proceedings of the 2014 ACM International Joint Conference on Pervasive and Ubiquitous Computing (UbiComp '14)*. ACM, New York. 897–908. DOI: 10.1145/2632048.2632062. 30

Veljko Pejovic, Neal Lathia, Cecilia Mascolo, and Mirco Musolesi. 2015. Mobile-based experience sampling for behaviour research. In *Emotions and Personality in Personalized Services*. Springer. https://arxiv.org/abs/1508.03725. 30

Peter Peltonen, Esko Kurvinen, Antti Salovaara, Giulio Jacucci, Tommi Ilmonen, John Evans, Antti Oulasvirta, and Petri Saarikko. 2008. It's mine, don't touch!: Interactions at a large multi-touch display in a city center. In *Proceedings of the SIGCHI Conference on Human Factors in Computing Systems (CHI '08)*. ACM, New York. 1285–1294. DOI: 10.1145/1357054.1357255. 4, 29

Jennifer Preece, Yvonne Rogers, and Helen Sharp. 2015. *Interaction Design: Beyond Human-Computer Interaction*, 4th Edition. Wiley. 3

Sara Price and Yvonne Rogers. 2004. Let's get physical: the learning benefits of interacting in digitally augmented physical spaces. In J.D.M. Underwood and J. Gardner (Eds.), *Computers and Education: Special Issue: 21st Century Learning*: 43, 137–151. DOI: 10.1016/j.compedu.2003.12.009. 43

Cliff Randell, Sara Price, Yvonne Rogers, Eric Harris, and Geraldine Fitzpatrick. 2004. The ambient horn: Designing a novel audio-based learning experience. *Personal and Ubiquitous Computing*, 8 (3-4), 177–183. DOI: 10.1007/s00779-004-0275-x. 40

Mitchel R. Resnick and Uri Wilensky. 1997. Diving into complexity: Developing probabilistic decentralized thinking through role-playing activities. *Journal of the Learning Sciences*, 7 (2), 153–172. 36

Yvonne Rogers. 1992. Ghosts in the network: Distributed troubleshooting in a shared environment. In *Proceedings of CSCW*. ACM, New York. DOI: 10.1145/143457.143546. 346–355. 17

Yvonne Rogers. 1993. Common-sense reasoning and everyday activities. *Pragmatics & Cognition*, 1 (2), 307–340. 14

Yvonne Rogers and Judi Ellis. 1994. Distributed cognition: an alternative framework for analysing and explaining collaborative working. *Journal of Information Technology*, 9 (2), 119–128. DOI: 10.1057/jit.1994.12. 17

Yvonne Rogers, Mike Scaife, Eric Harris, Ted Phelps, Sara Price, Hilary Smith, Henk Muller, Cliff Randell, Andrew Moss, Ian Taylor, Danae Stanton, Claire O'Malley, Greta Corke, and Silvia Gabrielli. 2002. Things aren't what they seem to be: innovation through technology inspiration. In *Proceedings of the 4th Conference on Designing Interactive Systems: Processes, Practices, Methods, and Techniques (DIS '02)*. ACM, New York. 373–378. DOI: 10.1145/778712.778766. 27

Yvonne Rogers, Sara Price, Geraldine Fitzpatrick, G, Rowanne Fleck, R., Eric Harris, Hilary Smith, H., Cliff Randell, Claire O'Malley, Danäe Stanton, Mark Thompson, M., and Mark Weal. 2004. Designing new forms of digital augmentation for learning outdoors. In *Proceedings of Third International Conference for Interaction Design and Children 2004*, ACM, New York, 3–10. DOI: 10.1145/1017833.1017834. 43

Yvonne Rogers, Sara Price, Cliff Randell, Danäe Stanton-Fraser, Mark Weal, and Geraldine Fitzpatrick. 2005. Ubi-learning integrates indoor and outdoor experiences. In *Communications of the ACM*. 48 (1), 55–59. DOI: 10.1145/1039539.1039570. 34, 35

Yvonne Rogers, Kay Connelly, Lenore Tedesco, William Hazlewood, Andrew Kurtz, Robert E Hall, Josh Hursey, and Tammy Toscos. 2007. Why it's worth the hassle: The value of *in-situ* studies when designing ubicomp. In J. Krumm, G. D. Abowd, A. Seneviratne., and T. Strang (Eds.) *UbiComp 2007: Ubiquitous Computing. UbiComp 2007. Lecture Notes in Computer Science*, vol 4717. Springer, Berlin, Heidelberg. 3, 7, 35, 45

Yvonne Rogers, William R. Hazlewood, Paul Marshall, Nick Dalton, and Susanna Hertrich. 2010. Ambient influence: can twinkly lights lure and abstract representations trigger behavioral change? In *Proceedings of the 12th ACM International Conference on Ubiquitous Computing (UbiComp '10)*. ACM, New York. 261–270. DOI: 10.1145/1864349.1864372. 21, 34, 47

Yvonne Rogers. 2011. Interaction design gone wild: striving for wild theory. *Interactions*, 18 (4), 58–62. DOI: 10.1145/1978822.1978834. 16, 30, 80

Yvonne Rogers. 2012. *HCI Theory: Classical, Modern, and Contemporary*. Synthesis Lectures on Human-Centered Informatics. Morgan & Claypool Publishers. DOI: 10.2200/S00418ED-1V01Y201205HCI014. x

Yvonne Rogers, Paul Marshall, and Nicola Yuill. 2013. Contrasting lab-based and in-the-wild studies for evaluating multi-user technologies. In *The Sage Handbook of Digital Technology Research*. 359-373. DOI: 10.4135/9781446282229.n24. 4

Yvonne Rogers and Gary Marsden. 2013. Does he take sugar?: moving beyond the rhetoric of compassion. *Interactions*, 20 (4), 48–57. DOI: 10.1145/2486227.2486238. 80

John Rooksby, Parvin Asadzadeh, Alistair Morrison, Claire McCallum, Cindy Gray, and Matthew Chalmers. 2016. Implementing ethics for a mobile app deployment. In *Proceedings of the 28th Australian Conference on Computer-Human Interaction (OzCHI '16)*. ACM, New York. 406–415. DOI: 10.1145/3010915.3010919. 77

Hasibullah Sahibzada, Eva Hornecker, Florian Echtler, and Patrick Tobias Fischer. 2017. Designing interactive advertisements for public displays. Full Paper. To appear in *CHI'2017, ACM*. 30

Mike Scaife and Yvonne Rogers. 1996. External cognition: how do graphical representations work? *International Journal of Human-Computer Studies*, 45 (2), 185–213. DOI: 10.1006/ijhc.1996.0048. 15

Denis Schleicher, Peter Jones, and Oksana Kachur. 2010. Bodystorming as embodied designing. *Interactions*, 17, 47–51. DOI: 10.1145/1865245.1865256. 24

Donald A. Schön. 1984. *The Reflective Practitioner: How Professionals Think in Action*. New York:Basic Books. 36

Abigail Sellen, Richard Harper, Rachel Eardley, Shahram Izadi, Tim Regan, Alex S. Taylor, and Ken R. Wood. 2006. HomeNote: supporting situated messaging in the home. In *Proceedings of the 2006 20th Anniversary Conference on Computer Supported Cooperative Work (CSCW '06)*. ACM, New York. 383–392. DOI: 10.1145/1180875.1180933. 24

Ben Shneiderman. 2011. Claiming success, charting the future: micro-HCI and macro-HCI. *Interactions*, 18 (5), 10-11. DOI: 10.1145/2008176.2008180. 80

Ben Shneiderman. 2016. *The New ABCs of Research: Achieving Breakthrough Collaborations*. Oxford University Press. 80

Eliot Soloway, Wayne Grant, Tinker, R., Jeremy Roschelle, Mills, M., Mitchel Resnick, Berg, R., and Mike Eisenberg. 1999. Science in the palms of their hands. *Communications of the ACM*, 42 (8), pp. 21–26. 35

Susan Leigh Star and James R. Griesemer. 1989. Institutional ecology, 'translations,' and boundary objects: Amateurs and professionals in Berkeley's Museum of Vertebrate Zoology, 1907–1939. *Social Studies of Science*, 19, 387–420. 23

Susan Leigh Star. 1999. The ethnography of infrastructure. *American Behavioral Scientist*, 43 (3), 377–391. DOI: 10.1177/00027649921955326. 28

Lucy A. Suchman. 1987. *Plans and Situated Action: The Problem of Human-Machine Communication.* Cambridge University Press. x, 11, 12

Nick Taylor, Keith Cheverst, Peter Wright, and Patrick Olivier. 2013. Leaving the wild: lessons from community technology handovers. In *Proceedings of the SIGCHI Conference on Human Factors in Computing Systems (CHI '13).* ACM, New York. 1549–1558. DOI: 10.1145/2470654.2466206. 1, 22, 23

Richard. H. Thaler and Cass. R. Sunstein. 2009. *Nudge: Improving Decisions About Health, Wealth and Happiness.* Penguin. 49

Peter Tolmie and Andy Crabtree. 2008. Deploying research technology in the home. In *Proceedings of the 2008 ACM Conference on Computer Supported Cooperative Work (CSCW '08).* ACM, New York. 639–648. DOI: 10.1145/1460563.1460662. 24

Janet van der Linden, Erwin Schoonderwaldt, Jon Bird, and Rose Johnson. 2011. MusicJacket—Combining motion capture and vibrotactile feedback to teach violin bowing. *IEEE Transactions on Instrumentation and Measurement*, 60 (1), 104–113. DOI: 10.1109/TIM.2010.2065770. DOI: 10.1109/TIM.2010.2065770. 4

Dave Ward and Mog Stapleton. 2012. Es are good: Cognition as enacted, embodied, embedded, affective and extended. In Fabio Paglieri (Ed.), *Consciousness in Interaction: The Role of the Natural and Social Context in Shaping Consciousness.* 89–104, John Benjamin Publishing Company. DOI: 10.1075/aicr.86.06war.

Peter Wang, Srinath Sibi, Brian Mok, and Wendy Ju. 2017. Marionette: Enabling on-road Wizard-of-Oz autonomous driving studies. In *Proceedings of the 2017 ACM/IEEE International Conference on Human-Robot Interaction (HRI '17).* ACM, New York. 234–243. DOI: 10.1145/2909824.3020256. 81

Mark J. Weal, Danius T. Michaelides, Mark K. Thompson, and David C. De Roure. 2003. Hypermedia in the ambient wood. *Hypermedia*, 9 (1), 137–156. DOI: 10.1080/13614560410001725347. 41

Mark Weiser. 1991. The computer for the twenty-first century. *Scientific American*, 94–10. 48

Danielle Wilde, Eric Harris, Yvonne Rogers, and Cliff Randell, C. 2003. The Periscope: supporting a computer-enhanced field trip for children. *Personal and Ubiquitous Computing*, 7, 227–233. DOI: 10.1007/s00779-003-0230-2. 39

Mary-Anne Williams, Xun Wang, Pramod Parajuli, Shaukat Abedi, Michelle Youssef, and Wei Wang. 2014. The fugitive: a robot in the wild. In *Proceedings of the 2014 ACM/IEEE International Conference on Human-Robot Interaction (HRI '14)*. ACM, New York. 111–111. DOI: 10.1145/2559636.2559653. 1

Johanna Ylipulli, Tiina Suopajärvi, Timo Ojala, Vassilis Kostakos, and Hannu Kukka (2014) Municipal WiFi and interactive displays: Appropriation of new technologies in public urban spaces. *Journal of Technological Forecasting and Social Change*, 89, 145–160. DOI: 10.1016/j.techfore.2013.08.037. 33

Nicola Yuill and Yvonne Rogers. 2012. Mechanisms for collaboration: A design and evaluation framework for multi-user interfaces. *ACM Transactions on Computer-Human Interactions*. 19 (1), Article 1 (May 2012), 25 pages. DOI: 10.1145/2147783.2147784. 45

Nicola Yuill and Alex Martin. 2016. Curling up with a good E-Book: Mother-child shared story reading on screen or paper affects embodied interaction and warmth. *Frontiers in Psychology*. DOI: 10.3389/fpsyg.2016.01951. 18

John Zimmerman, Jodi Forlizzi, and Shelley Evenson. 2007. Research through design as a method for interaction design research in HCI. In *Proceedings of the SIGCHI Conference on Human Factors in Computing Systems (CHI '07)*. ACM, New York. 493–502. DOI: 10.1145/1240624.1240704. 21

Author Biographies

Yvonne Rogers is the director of the Interaction Centre at UCL (UCLIC), and a deputy head of the Computer Science department at UCL. Her research interests lie at the intersection of physical computing, interaction design, and human-computer interaction. Much of her work is situated in the wild—concerned with informing, building and evaluating novel user experiences through creating and assembling a diversity of technologies (e.g., tangibles, Internet of Things) that augment everyday, learning, community engagement and collaborative work activities. She has been instrumental in promulgating new theories (e.g., external cognition), alternative methodologies (e.g., in the wild studies), and far-reaching research agendas (e.g., "Being Human: HCI in 2020" manifesto), and has pioneered an approach to innovation and ubiquitous learning. She has published over 250 articles, including her Morgan & Claypool monograph *HCI Theory: Classical, Modern and Contemporary*. She is a co-author of the definitive textbook on *Interaction Design and HCI* now published in its 4th edition that has sold over 150,000 copies worldwide and has been translated into 6 languages. She is a fellow of the BCS and the ACM CHI Academy.

Paul Marshall is a senior lecturer in interaction design at University College London. He received his DPhil from the University of Sussex and a BSc from the University of Edinburgh. From 2011 to 2012 he was a research fellow at the University of Warwick, and from 2006–2010 was a research fellow at the Open University Pervasive Interaction Lab. His research interests center on the design and evaluation of technologies that extend and augment individual human capabilities in the wild. This has included work on physical interaction and tangible interfaces; on technologies for face-to-face collaboration; on the design of technologies to fit specific physical contexts; and on extended cognition and perception. A recent focus has been on how communities and individuals use data for better understanding or well-being.